FACILITATOR'S GUIDE FOR IMAP
Integrating Mathematics and Pedagogy

FACILITATOR'S GUIDE FOR IMAP

INTEGRATING MATHEMATICS AND PEDAGOGY

*Searchable Collection of
Children's-Mathematical-Thinking
Video Clips*

RANDOLPH PHILIPP
San Diego State University

BONNIE SCHAPPELLE
San Diego State University

Boston • Columbus • Indianapolis • New York • San Francisco • Upper Saddle River
Amsterdam • Cape Town • Dubai • London • Madrid • Milan • Munich • Paris • Montreal • Toronto
Delhi • Mexico City • Sao Paulo • Sydney • Hong Kong • Seoul • Singapore • Taipei • Tokyo

Acquisitions Editor: Kelly Villella Canton
Editorial Assistant: Annalea Manalili
Marketing Manager: Danae April
Production Editor: Gregory Erb
Editorial Production Service: Omegatype Typography, Inc.
Manufacturing Buyer: Megan Cochran
Electronic Composition: Omegatype Typography, Inc.
Cover Designer: Jennifer Hart

10 9 8 7 6 5 4 3 2 1   BRG   15 14 13 12 11

www.pearsonhighered.com

ISBN-10: 0-13-209940-3
ISBN-13: 978-0-13-209940-0

Contents

PART I

Video of Children's Mathematical Thinking: An Overview

About Children's Thinking and Linking to IMAP

One of the most beautiful and powerful experiences teachers have is to observe children making sense of mathematics. Furthermore, when encouraged to approach mathematics in sense-making ways, children do exhibit rich understanding and creativity in their mathematics. If all students in the United States were experiencing mathematics as a rich, creative, and sense-making endeavor, this product would not be necessary. However, we know that such is not the case. News reports are replete with examples of the shortcomings in the teaching of mathematics in U.S. schools, and elementary school children in the United States are generally not developing acceptable levels of mathematical proficiency (National Center for Education Statistics, 1999).

During the past generation, a great deal of research has helped educators understand how people think and learn, and we have developed a better understanding for children's ways of thinking about mathematics and how children's ways of thinking differ from adults' thinking (National Research Council, 1999; 2001). As part of a large-scale National Science Foundation Research and Development study titled *Integrating Mathematics and Pedagogy (IMAP)*, we undertook research to determine whether infusing children's mathematical thinking earlier into the undergraduate mathematics preparation of prospective elementary school teachers might affect the mathematical content knowledge and belief development of teachers. We found that it did. (For information about our project, see our website at www.sci.sdsu.edu/CRMSE/IMAP/main .html).But as important as learning about children's mathematical thinking is for prospective teachers, it may be even more powerful for practicing teachers. Wilson and Berne (1999) documented that professional development based on children's thinking has helped teachers create rich instructional environments that promote mathematical inquiry and understanding, leading to documented improvement in student achievement. Using children's mathematical thinking in professional development contexts can motivate and promote growth in teachers' content knowledge of mathematics. Most elementary school teachers care, fundamentally, about children, not mathematics. Starting with children's thinking can therefore motivate prospective and practicing teachers to engage in mathematical discussions by helping them realize that to understand and nurture the depth and variety in this thinking, they themselves must grapple with the mathematics inherent in the varied strategies that children use to solve problems.

Our purpose for creating this product is to provide teachers with opportunities to grapple with issues of mathematics teaching and learning when they arise in the context of children's mathematical thinking. From thousands of video clips of children's mathematical thinking that we have collected, we selected 232 that capture a range of elementary school children's mathematical reasoning. The video clips in this product were selected because they clearly highlight children's mathematical thinking, and because the sound quality is excellent and complete transcripts of all interviews are included, salient aspects of the children's solutions are evident in every video clip. (In rare cases in which voices are inaudible, the words are superimposed on the video.) Most video clips are of interviews of individual children; some of the interviews were conducted by experts whereas others were conducted by prospective teachers who had no such relevant experience. In addition to the clips of individual children, several clips show a small group of children or a whole class.

What Is Children's Mathematical Thinking? Why Focus on It?

Children's Mathematical Thinking

The term *children's mathematical thinking* contains three distinct words, each of which we unpack below.

Children's Mathematical Thinking

The students shown in these clips are at the K–6 levels. The children are ethnically, linguistically, socioeconomically, and cognitively diverse, but, more important, we view all these students as enthusiastically sharing their thinking with us. Some children were selected because they were or have learned in particularly strong meaning-making classrooms, whereas other children are enrolled in more traditional classrooms.

Children's *Mathematical* Thinking

Mathematical Proficiency

By *mathematics* we mean the five strands of the model of mathematical proficiency (National Research Council, 2001): understanding concepts; knowing how and when to apply procedures; problem solving; reasoning mathematically and justifying one's reasoning; and believing that mathematics is worthwhile and that one can, with steady effort, learn mathematics (see Figure 1). Seldom is the focus on these clips about applying a rote procedure; instead, most of the interviewers are guided by an image of mathematics as a sense-making endeavor. (Note that the product includes search terms, one of which is *novice interviewers,* shown in 13 clips. Even in the cases when novices, such as college students, conducted interviews, they were supported so that they strove to understand the children's thinking. However, because they were novices, they should not be expected to have delved as deeply as expert interviewers would do.)

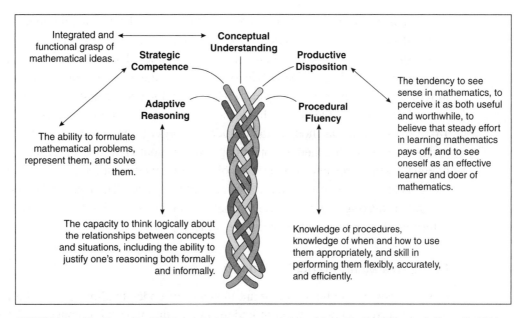

FIGURE 1.   The Strands of Mathematical Proficiency (adapted from National Research Council, 2001, p. 117).

Knowledge for Teaching Mathematics

Teachers are professionals, and one defining characteristic of professionals is that they hold specialized knowledge different from knowledge that laypeople hold (National Research Council, 1999). Two essential types of knowledge teachers need to know to be prepared to teach mathematics for understanding are mathematical content knowledge and pedagogical content knowledge. Mathematical content knowledge has been subdivided into *common content knowledge,* the mathematical knowledge teachers are responsible for developing in students, and *specialized content knowledge,* the mathematical knowledge that is used in teaching, but not directly taught to students (Ball, Hill, & Bass, 2005). These two types of content knowledge are distinguished from *pedagogical content knowledge (PCK),* "the ways of representing and formulating the subject that make it comprehensible to others" (Shulman, 1986, p. 9), including, for example, students' conceptions. We provide an example of each knowledge type related to whole number division. Evaluating and understanding the meaning of 20 ÷ 4 is common content knowledge, whereas the ability to write a real-life story problem that could be represented by the expression 20 ÷ 4 is specialized content knowledge. A teacher with pedagogical content knowledge about whole number division would realize that primary-grades children asked to solve a partitive-division problem (e.g., "How many jelly beans would each child get if we shared 20 jelly beans equally among 4 children?") generally model the problem by dealing out the 20 among 4 groups and that the answer is the number in each group.

Although pedagogical content knowledge (PCK) is different from and extends beyond mathematical content knowledge, PCK clearly rests upon a solid mathematical foundation. When teachers learn to attend to students' mathematical thinking, they develop more effective ways of interacting with and making sense of their students' thinking, and they also extend their understanding of the mathematics. That is, learning about students' mathematical thinking can lead teachers to a deeper understanding of mathematics, which in turn can better prepare a teacher to listen to and support her students' reasoning. For example, consider a student who holds the common misconception that 1/8 is greater than 1/6. A teacher who has thought about students' ways of thinking might be prepared to respond to the child that there *is* something *greater* about eighths than sixths—the number of equal-sized pieces into which the whole is partitioned—but the number of equal-sized pieces is inversely related to the size of each of the pieces. The teacher can see the sense the child is making while also seeing what the child is *not* understanding, and the teacher is then in a better position to support the student.

Children's Mathematical *Thinking*

Correct answers can be an important indicator of understanding, but at times, students arrive at correct answers without understanding the underlying concepts. These video clips are focused more upon the ways that the students think than upon the answers. Attention is paid to the types of reasoning students apply, and the video clips highlight details of children's use of manipulatives, fingers, and drawings, and whenever possible, children are asked to explain their reasoning.

Connections to Cognitively Guided Instruction

One particularly influential line of research and professional development is known as Cognitively Guided Instruction (CGI) (Carpenter, Fennema, Franke, Levi, & Empson, 1999; Carpenter & Moser, 1984). CGI is based upon the principle that students possess informal knowledge on which instruction might be based, and the more teachers learn about children's mathematical thinking, the more effectively teachers might extend children's knowledge. CGI draws upon frameworks for problem types and children's solution strategies, and although this video collection draws upon this work, we do not explicitly include the problem types or solutions strategies. This product is based upon the same philosophy as CGI, and we are confident that teachers who find CGI useful will also find this video product useful. However, this video collection was not developed just for teachers familiar with CGI. Instead, this product has been developed so as to be useful to anyone interested in issues related to K–6 mathematics teaching and learning.

A Stance Toward Teaching Mathematics

In the United States, opportunities for sustained professional development are not built into the professional lives of teachers. This condition is unfortunate because although teachers continue to grow from experience, research has shown that teachers, even those with many years of experience, when provided thoughtful and sustained professional development opportunities, can transform their teaching. Furthermore, we are not confident that this situation will change in the near future.

Teaching as Learning (An Inquiry Stance)

Perhaps the single most important stance that teachers learn to take is to continue to learn from their own practices. This perspective has been referred to as a stance of inquiry. Lamb, Philipp, Jacobs, and Schappelle (2009) wrote,

> Practices that provide evidence of an inquiry stance include learning to question one's own and others' assumptions and beliefs about teaching, learning, and schooling; taking a critical stance on the work of others; and not accepting scripted materials or research as the final word on what teachers should do. Wells (1999) wrote that an inquiry stance also indicates "a willingness to wonder, to ask questions, and to seek to understand by collaborating with others in the attempt to make answers to them" (p.121). Cochran-Smith and Lytle (1999, 2001) stated that teachers with an inquiry stance look more deeply than at test scores or correct answers for evidence of student learning; they may look for other indicators of students' understandings, including what students say and how they reason about problems or questions. It is the development of genuine curiosity about their own teaching and their own students coupled with the development of lenses for answering those questions about which they are curious that makes the development of an inquiry stance powerful. (p. 17)

Although we see no royal road to developing a stance of inquiry toward one's teaching, a particularly promising approach is to learn to focus upon the mathematical reasoning of one's students.

Children's Mathematical Thinking: The Teacher's Path Through the Mathematical Terrain on an Inquiry Journey

When teachers learn to focus in more nuanced ways on their students' mathematical thinking and develop a students' thinking lens, they begin to see the mathematical content in two ways: as a teacher and as a student. For example, in the diagram in Figure 2, they understand that the shaded portion is one eighth of a whole circle and one fourth of half of a circle. Furthermore, when a student incorrectly states that the shaded region is one fifth of a circle, the teacher not only anticipates this response but also understands that in some contexts the child's response makes sense. For example, most people would consider a baby to represent one fifth of the people living in a home with her parents and two older siblings.

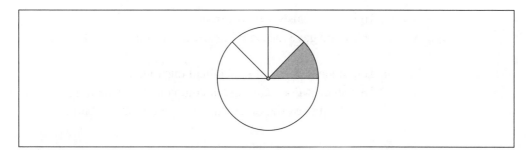

FIGURE 2.   One fourth of one half is one eighth of the whole.

A children's-thinking focus opens a rich and fascinating world to a teacher because she has access to creative, thoughtful, and fresh ways of thinking. But the benefits go beyond understanding children: Teachers may also grapple with mathematics as a result. For example, many teachers think of the diagram in Figure 2 as representing 1/8. (Note here that no unit is specified for the fraction.) However, when the teacher begins to understand the difficulties her students have with the changing unit during fractions work, she may emphasize the need for students to think and speak more clearly. In this case, the shaded region might, simultaneously, be 1/8 (of a whole), 1/4 (of a half), 1/2 (of a fourth), 2 (of a sixteenth), and even 1 of 5 (unequal) pieces. Furthermore, although different, these conceptions are equally valid! Is it any wonder that students struggle with rational numbers?

Teachers who have come to focus on children's thinking find that they begin to think in more subtle, nuanced ways. Recently, a teacher said that in the past, she often felt discouraged and would walk to lunch feeling that her students "just didn't get it." She said that she went home feeling as if she was "an awful teacher today." However, when she came to better understood how to listen to her students, she began to view teaching from a problem-solving perspective. Her views of teaching changed, and she replaced "my students are not getting it" or "I was an awful teacher today" with "parts of this lesson were unsuccessful. How can I modify the lesson to improve it?" The notion that "teaching elementary mathematics is generally easy (I explain, they listen, and then they practice, but my goodness, this is boring!), so why am I having so much difficulty" is slowly replaced with "teaching mathematics is challenging and difficult (I pose a problem, they explain, we all listen to understand various ways of thinking). This process is complicated, but my goodness, I love it, and so do they!"

When teachers change their views of themselves or their students, they also think more subtly about specific aspects of teaching and learning. For example, whereas a teacher at one point will see only a wrong answer when a child says that the shaded region in Figure 2 represents 1/4, the same teacher, after focusing on children's thinking, will see 1/4 as the correct answer to a different question (What fraction of the top half of the circle is shaded?). Below are pairs of comments that might represent a teacher's thinking before, and many years after, beginning to focus on children's mathematical thinking.

Before: This child is right (or wrong).
After: This child is thinking about this in this way... ,

Before: This child's answer is incorrect.
After: This child gave the right answer to a different question.

Before: This student does not understand this topic.
After: This student does not have a complete understanding. How is she thinking? What does she understand on which I might build?

Before: This student understands this idea.
After: This student seems to understand this idea in this context. Where might I take her? What question might I pose to extend the child's understanding?

Before: I am a _____ (good, bad) mathematics teacher.
After: I am becoming a better mathematics teacher. I am growing!

Before: Whatever I expect, my students disappoint me. They just don't get it.
After: Because I was expecting the wrong things for my students, what I thought
          were high expectations were actually the wrong expectations. Now I see
          that they know so much more, and because I know how to tap into what
          they know, my expectations of students are much higher than before and
          are more often met.

When teachers assume a stance of inquiry that focuses on children's mathematical thinking, they often transition from listening to a student to determine whether he is right, to listening to determine whether the child is sharing the correct reasoning, to listening to understand what reasoning the child is using. In the first state, the teacher does not consider the reasoning at all; in the second state, she tries to get students to reason in her particular way; in the third state, she recognizes that, fundamentally, mathematics is a sense-making endeavor and, even more important, that helping students reason in privileged ways is supporting students to reason in sense-making ways.

Learning to *Notice* Differently

Instruction that builds on children's mathematical thinking has been endorsed in several reform documents (National Council of Teachers of Mathematics [NCTM], 2000; National Research Council [NRC], 2001). Teaching by building on students thinking requires "sizing up students' ideas and responding" (Ball, Lubienski, & Mewborn, 2001, p. 453), but listening to students' thinking in such a way that teachers may respond to effectively support student thinking is challenging and requires teachers to learn to attend differently to what their students say and do. For example, consider the following brief teacher/student interaction:

Teacher: How much is six plus seven?
Kyle: Twelve.
Teacher: Kyle, how much is six plus six?
Kyle: Oh, I see. No, it is 13.

Kyle answered both questions incorrectly, but he understood that the teacher's second question served the purpose of asking him to reflect upon the first response, and realizing that 6 plus 6 is 12, he reconsidered his answer to 6 plus 7. Now consider the teacher's role. When Kyle responded, "Twelve," the teacher assumed that he might know 6 plus 6, so she followed up with the relevant question. Teacher noticing is a relatively new and exciting construct in mathematics education (Sherin, Jacobs, & Philipp, 2011), and the previous interaction captures three essential aspects of a teacher's noticing. First, the teacher *attended* to Kyle's response; that is, she listened not only to hear whether Kyle answered correctly but also attended to the incorrect answer Kyle provided. Second, she *interpreted* Kyle's incorrect response through her lens of children's mathematical thinking. In this case, she analyzed Kyle's incorrect response by drawing upon her experience that students tend to learn their doubles (4 + 4; 5 + 5; 6 + 6, etc.) before learning other number facts, and she used this understanding to make sense of Kyle's thinking. Third, she *decided how to respond* to Kyle so as to support his reasoning, in this case by posing the question to which Kyle had correctly responded.

This example highlights the three components referred to as "teachers' professional noticing of children's mathematical thinking" (Jacobs, Lamb, & Philipp, 2010): *attending, interpreting,* and *deciding how to respond.*

Attending

We all realize that two people seldom *see* the same things in the same way, even when looking at the same event, but many may be surprised to learn that even trained professionals often differ on what they see. Because teachers are constantly faced with making sense of the *"blooming, buzzing confusion of sensory data"* (Sherin & Star, 2011, p. 69) they face in the classroom, they differ in that to which they attend. Even teachers with many years of experience may notice very different aspects of the classroom. However, as teachers learn more about their students' thinking, they are able to identify and distinguish relevant details about children's mathematical thinking from not-so-important details (Jacobs et al., 2010), listening in more nuanced and sophisticated ways. That is, they *see* differently.

Interpreting

Teachers' beliefs and knowledge affect not only to *what* they attend in the classroom but also *how* they interpret what they see. In the example above, most teachers would observe that Kyle gave an incorrect sum for 6 plus 7, but they might differ on their interpretations. The teacher in the example drew upon her understanding of students' thinking to consider what Kyle might have understood and then posed a subsequent question, whereas another teacher might simply conclude that Kyle needs more practice with his facts and move on to someone else or to another problem.

When we make observations, we often attend to and interpret almost simultaneously, especially in a complex classroom environment. We have found that the more teachers learn about students' thinking, the more sophisticated their interpretations become. We have also found that video is an effective medium for supporting teachers while they learn to observe differently. When watching video, teachers need not immediately respond to students. Furthermore, video may be paused and rewatched, providing teachers with opportunities to consider alternative interpretations. For example, when watching video, a teacher may observe a child who answers incorrectly and may interpret that the child is confused or that the teacher was not doing her job. But she may also see that the child understands something, and she may consider the challenges faced by the teacher. These are two different, and arguably valid, interpretations.

No one can observe video in a completely objective manner because we all have our perspectives and biases. However, we have found that the more teachers confront the biases that color what they observe, the more clearly they are able to distinguish between what actually happened and their evaluation of what happened. When teachers learn to delay making judgments about video, they become more objective observers of classroom interactions and are thereby enabled to focus upon children's and teachers' thinking. Consider the following three descriptions of the same video clip (Mason, 2011):

A. "the moment the teacher entered and dominated the two children"
B. "the moment the teacher entered [the shot] and started talking, standing behind the two children who were slouched on the table"
C. "the moment the teacher entered [the shot] and started talking, standing behind the two children who had their arms on the table, their heads resting on their arms, and who were looking up at the teacher"

The use of the word *dominated* in the first description is judgmental, and though the second description is less judgmental, the term *slouched* also contains evaluative judgment. One test of whether a description contains fewer judgments and interpretations is the extent to which all viewers agree on "just the facts." The third description is the most precise description, and being void of inferences, this description "is more easily identified by someone spinning through the video and more easily recognized, both by people who have seen the video and more generally as an incident within most teachers' experience" (Mason, 2011).

Deciding How to Respond

Fundamentally, teachers are responsible for supporting students' mathematical learning, and to accomplish this goal, they need to focus on students' reasoning and make decisions on the basis of that reasoning. Teachers vary dramatically in terms of the extent to which they attend to students' mathematical thinking when deciding how to respond, with some teachers focusing robustly on students' thinking and others showing little or no evidence that students' thinking would affect the in-the-moment classroom decisions they would make (Jacobs et al., 2010). One question we have found particularly helpful for supporting teachers while they learn to focus on students' thinking when watching video is "What question might the teacher pose next?" This question is challenging because it requires that teachers focus on the mathematical goals for the lesson, the student's understanding, and various ways that the teacher might connect these two. But by isolating a teaching moment and focusing on the teacher's choices, teachers answering this question can explicitly consider the various ways they may focus their attention when teaching.

How Do Teachers Benefit From Using Video of Children's Mathematical Thinking?

When working with other teachers who have used video, consider making, with their input, a list of the benefits of using video. Below is a list compiled from several presentations to teachers, some of whom are professional developers, who have used video, some extensively, with other teachers.

Video

1. enables one to have an objective viewpoint—one can stand back and see differently;

2. can raise teachers' expectations of what students can do;
3. may be stopped, rewatched, edited, and so on;
4. provides opportunities for us as teachers to be critically reflective—we can see our actions in others.
5. enables us to watch many examples of instruction but is less threatening and easier logistically than entering one another's classrooms;
6. provides us opportunities to see that children's approaches to mathematics and mathematical thinking differ from adults' approaches;
7. enables us to watch the same person over time;
8. can be used as a basis for discussion of next steps;
9. enables us to model questioning techniques in a safe way;
10. is efficient; video can be used out of school; it can provide opportunities to quickly raise complex issues.

When in the act of teaching, teachers must attend to the *"blooming, buzzing confusion of sensory data"* (Sherin, and Star, 2011, p.69), constantly acting and reacting so as to move the lesson along while addressing all the content and management issues that naturally arise in classrooms. Video can slow this process—even stop it—and enable one to rewatch it. With video, teachers can consider an isolated instructional moment, stop the video, and take a side trip to consider more deeply or innovatively a mathematical issue, a student comment, or a choice of representation or other pedagogical consideration. But video can also be chosen to address the complexity of a classroom. In other words, in using video, one has choices.

PART II

Using This Product

An Important Note About Professionalism and Respect

These video clips were developed for use with prospective and practicing teachers, and although practicing teachers have extensive teaching experience that prospective teachers do not, we have found that even experienced teachers generally do not have opportunities to use video as a source of professional development. Therefore we highly recommend that before using these video clips, facilitators discuss their respectful use.

All people on these video clips graciously agreed to be included on video media that are to be used for educational purposes. When viewing a child who seems confused, please do not focus blame on the child or, for that matter, on his or her teacher. Rather, try to understand what sense the child is or is not making and try to understand the circumstances that may have led to this child's becoming confused. Help prospective and practicing teachers consider what they would need to know to provide children with opportunities to develop deeper and richer mathematical understanding. We want to protect not only the children and teachers in these video clips but also the teachers who view them. If teachers approach these video clips by blaming students or teachers, they are more likely to become frustrated by and apprehensive about their own developing knowledge of mathematics and learning. If instead they approach the video clips with an orientation toward understanding and reflecting upon mathematics and mathematical learning, they may enhance their view of teachers as being part of a community who learn and develop together. They may come to see that effective mathematics teachers develop their craft over a long period of time by reflecting upon both the mathematics they are teaching and the ways that children are engage with the mathematics. Furthermore, when they develop a stance of inquiry toward their own teaching and learning, they will see themselves on a professional journey of growth and will be more accepting of the fact that they may not yet be where they would like to be on this journey. But so long as they are learning, they can accept where they are!

Four Emergent Principles From the Video

This product contains 232 video clips, and by combining clips, many principles about mathematics, teaching, and learning may be illustrated. Below are four principles that we have found to be particularly important to highlight when working with prospective or practicing teachers.

Principle 1. *The way most students are learning mathematics in the United States is problematic. In particular, students learn to manipulate mathematical symbols without developing the underlying conceptual meanings for the symbols.*

With the persistent news stories in the popular press reporting students' difficulties with mathematics, one might assume that everyone in the United States is aware that we have a problem with our students' learning of mathematics. However, many prospective teachers are simply unaware of the depth of the problem, and until they understand the problem, they have little motivation for considering that the way they learned mathematics may not be the way they need to learn to teach mathematics.

Furthermore, although many practicing teachers are aware that many U.S. students are not learning mathematics, many either do not believe that we have a major problem or define the problem solely as a failure to effectively teach symbol manipulation.

Data from reports such as the National Assessment of Educational Progress (NAEP) consistently show that students in the United States are failing to understand the mathematics they are being taught. For example, Figure 1 shows a fraction-estimation task and the results for 13-year-old students in the United States (Carpenter, Corbitt, Kepner, Lindquist, & Reys, 1980). When discussing this item, teachers are generally surprised to find that fewer than 25% of the students in middle school are able to estimate fraction size.

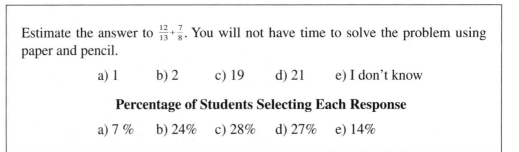

Estimate the answer to $\frac{12}{13} + \frac{7}{8}$. You will not have time to solve the problem using paper and pencil.

a) 1   b) 2   c) 19   d) 21   e) I don't know

Percentage of Students Selecting Each Response

a) 7 %   b) 24%   c) 28%   d) 27%   e) 14%

FIGURE 1.   NAEP item and percentage of 13-year-old students selecting each response.

An effective means of addressing Principle 1 is to have teachers interview, or view video clips of, children. Carefully constructed interviews of intermediate-grades children (note that sample interviews are included in the resources section of the video, and Story 6 includes guidance related to interviewing) are generally effective for demonstrating that many children lack conceptual understanding of fractions; however, teachers can also come to see this problem by viewing and discussing carefully selected video clips. Many of the video clips in this collection highlight Principle 1. One example (Clip #302) shows a bright, articulate student named Ally, identified by her teacher as an average fifth grader from a class in a high-performing school; Ally struggled to make sense of fractions. In the video clip, Ally explained her reasoning for comparing fractions, and within one minute, on three consecutive comparison tasks, Ally's explanations highlight three common fraction conceptions that often lead to students' incorrect reasoning. On one task she explained that 1 is bigger than 4/3 "because 1 is a whole number." On the next task she explained that 1/2 is greater than 3/6 because "if you change the denominator [of 1/2] to 1, just one digit lower, then it would equal to 1, and 1 is a whole number." On the subsequent task, she explained that 1/7 is greater than 2/7 because "I wasn't quite sure about this one, so I chose one seventh because I thought it was just the smallest number, and usually you go down to the smallest number to get to the biggest number [in fractions]." (This video clip is incorporated into Story 4, a series of video clips showing that middle school students struggle to understand fractions and clips to show how young children can build on their informal understanding to develop fraction understanding.)

Understanding the depth of the problem with how mathematics is being learned by most students requires us to delve more deeply into the nature of Ally's reasoning. Three conceptions driving Ally's thinking are evident in this 1-minute span of the video clip: (a) fractions are less than 1; (b) fractions can be compared by comparing the differences between the numerators and the denominators; and (c) with fractions, the number that looks larger is smaller. All three conceptions were valid ways of reasoning at one point in students' mathematical experiences. Ally's first conception, that fractions are less than 1, has its roots in the initial introduction to fractions when students learn that fractions are parts of a whole and, hence, must be less than the whole. The fraction language commonly used reinforces this conception when, for example, students conceptualize 3/4 as "three out of four." Does it make sense, in this context, to consider "five out of four"?[1] The residue of conceptualizing fractions as less than 1 is evident in our commonly used language, when, for example, we say, "I completed only a fraction of the job." The technique of comparing fractions by determining the differences between numerators and denominators yields correct answers when constrained to positive fractions less than 1 with equal denominators (or numerators). For example, one could correctly conclude that 7/9 is greater than 4/9 because the difference between 9 and 7 is less than the difference between 9 and 4. The third conception, that larger numbers result in smaller values, yields correct answers in comparison of unit fractions. For many years students learned that 8 is larger than 6, but then, for fractions, 1/8 is smaller than 1/6. When teachers begin to understand students' reasoning, they can develop more nuanced understandings and, for example, come to view the statement that "you go down to the smallest number to get to the biggest number" as one that makes sense in some contexts but not in others.

Principle 2. *Understanding concepts is more powerful and more generative than memorizing procedures.*

Principle 1 highlights a problem with many students' learning of mathematics in the United States. Principle 2 presents one path for considering how to support students: Seek ways to connect new ideas to students' informal conceptual understanding.

---

[1] The language "three out of four" is associated with another difficulty for students. Students think of "3 out of 4" as literally meaning that 3 parts of the 4 have been removed, and these students conclude, for example, that 1/7 is greater than 2/7 because for 1/7 they are removing only 1 of 7 from the whole whereas for 2/7 they are removing 2 of 7 from the whole. Perhaps this is the reasoning that Ally applied when concluding, although she "wasn't quite sure," that 1/7 was greater than 2/7. Note that given the *out of* conception, this reasoning, although mathematically incorrect, is understandable and consistent.

For example, teachers are often surprised to discover that many primary-grades children can solve multiplication and division problems when the problems are embedded in real-life contexts. Consider the problem *"Tad had 15 guppies. He put 3 guppies in each jar. How many jars did Tad put guppies in?"* Many adults think that because they view this problem as division, primary-grades children cannot solve it because they have yet to learn about division. When teachers learn that more than 70% of kindergarten children in one study were able to solve this problem at the end of the year (Carpenter, Ansell, Franke, Fennema, & Weisbeck, 1993), they are surprised. Perhaps even more surprising to teachers is children's success at solving the problem *"Nineteen children are taking a mini-bus to the zoo. They will have to sit either 2 or 3 to a seat. The bus has 7 seats. How many children will have to sit 3 to a seat, and how many can sit 2 to a seat?"* At the end of the year, among students who had been in classrooms in which the focus had been to teach mathematics meaningfully, more than half the kindergarten students correctly solved this problem. Note that this is a two-variable problem of the type often used in middle- or high-school algebra classes. Learning concepts had enabled these students to make sense of complex, even multistep, problems.

An effective means for highlighting Principle 2 is to arrange for teachers to interview or to observe video clips of primary-grades children because young children often understand and approach mathematics in meaning-making ways. One video clip that effectively highlights Principle 2 shows a student, Felisha, who correctly added 3/4 + 1/2 at the end of second grade although she had not yet learned any procedures for adding fractions (Clip #329). Felisha had spent seven mornings learning fractions with three other children of the same age from a teacher who approached the teaching of fractions by posing real-life, equal-sharing situations. Because Felisha had developed rich understanding of partitioning and equivalence, she was able to flexibly approach fraction tasks.

Principle 3. *The ways children reason about mathematics are varied and diverse and generally differ from the ways that adults think.*

Although most teachers recognize *"Maria has 6 shells. How many more shells does Maria need to collect so that she'll have 13 shells altogether?"* as a missing-addend problem, they are not always aware of the various approaches students use when left to solve the problem in ways that make sense to them. Some children solve this problem by counting out 6 counters, then counting up to 13 counters, and then counting the 7 that they added. A more sophisticated solution involves children's starting with the first quantity, 6, "in their heads," counting on to 13 on their fingers, and noting that the answer is the number of extended fingers. In a still more sophisticated strategy, one that does not involve counting, a child uses a fact she knows, 6 + 6 = 12, to infer that because 13 is 1 more than 12, the answer must be 7, 1 more than 6 (Carpenter et al., 1999). These solutions approaches appear in many of the video clips, and three in particular might be used together because they show three children solving the same problem differently (Clips #187, #177, and #173).

A second video example that effectively highlights Principle 3 is of Javier, a fifth-grade student, determining how many eggs are in six dozen. Javier reasoned that 5 times

12 is 60, and 12 more is 72, so there are 72 eggs in six dozen. When asked how he knew that 5 times 12 is 60, Javier, a recent immigrant to the United States from Mexico, responded in his second language, "Because 12 times 10 equals 120. If I take the half of 120, that would be 60" (Clip #158).

Principle 4. *Elementary school mathematics is not elementary.*

A common belief among lay people is that the content of elementary school mathematics is simple; however, when teachers learn more about children's mathematical thinking, they begin to realize that engaging deeply with issues of mathematics and mathematics teaching and learning, at any grade level, is complex. For example, although adults may remember the procedure commonly taught for dividing fractions, few people, even few mathematics majors, can explain why, when we divide fractions, we invert and multiply. Teachers need two types of mathematical knowledge: They need to know and understand the content that they will teach to children, but they also need to hold a deeper understanding if they are to attend to their students' ways of reasoning. A distinction drawn in the literature is between *common content knowledge,* the mathematical knowledge teachers are responsible for developing in students, and *specialized content knowledge,* the mathematical knowledge that is used in teaching but not directly taught to students (Ball et al., 2005). For example, the procedure used for dividing $1\frac{1}{2}$ by 1/3 is common content knowledge taught to students, but a deeper understanding of the mathematical issues raised by trying to understand how students make sense of fraction division is part of the specialized content knowledge teachers need to teach mathematics to children.

One source for highlighting Principle 4 is to arrange for teachers to interview children or observe video clips of children solving problems. A video clip that effectively highlights Principle 4 shows Elliot, a sixth-grade student, solving two division tasks. Elliot solves the first task, 1 ÷ 1/3, by correctly reasoning that three 1/3s make one whole. Elliot is then asked to solve $1\frac{1}{2}$ ÷ 1/3. He again correctly reasons that because three 1/3s make 1 and 1/2 has another 1/3, there are four 1/3s in $1\frac{1}{2}$. He also correctly determines that after removing four 1/3s from $1\frac{1}{2}$, 1/6 remains. However, Elliot's final answer is incorrect because instead of reconceptualizing the 1/6 as 1/2 of 1/3 and answering that there are $4\frac{1}{2}$ one-thirds in $1\frac{1}{2}$, he leaves the 1/6 as a remainder but treats it as a quotient when incorrectly answering $4\frac{1}{6}$ (Clip #321).

This video clip highlights that mathematical understanding is seldom either complete or nonexistent but is, instead, held in degrees (the theme of Story 3); although students usually understand some aspects of a concept (in this case, that $a \div b$ may be thought of as "How many bs are in a?"), they may be struggling with other aspects of the concept (for Elliot, that the remainder may be reconceptualized as part of the quotient). This principle, curiously, applies to all learners, and when we discuss this as a principle of learning, teachers begin to see that instead of viewing their conceptual holes as weaknesses, they may view them as a natural part of engaging with a rich domain and that, hence, they need to be open to continuing to learn throughout their lives, including from their students.

Using Video and Written Student Work:
A Conjectured Sequence

At times a facilitator may choose to show a video clip with little or no preparation. For example, to highlight that girls of color can engage innovatively with mathematics, one might show Clip #207 or #325, or to demonstrate that first graders can solve multiplication or division problems, one might show Clips #127 and #132. However, in general, we suggest that teachers grapple with the mathematics of a video clip prior to viewing the clip and then consider the problem from a student's perspective. Teachers who think about a problem, both from their own perspectives and from a student's perspective, before they see the problem solved in the video clip are poised to attend to details of the video that they would otherwise miss.

Each video clip is accompanied by a Word document containing the problem posed and supporting questions. These documents were designed to support facilitators in helping teachers consider the mathematics and children's thinking about the mathematics. Furthermore, because complete transcripts are available for each clip (different from the transcript synchronized to the video), facilitators may select transcript portions for analysis by teachers. Finally, many clips have associated jpeg files containing one screen shot; some of these may be used to support discussion.

Figure 3 provides a sequence of three steps we suggest facilitators consider when using video with teachers.

---

1. **Teachers consider the mathematics.**
   - Ask teachers to solve the problem in two ways, and discuss their approaches.

2. **Teachers consider students' thinking.**
   - Ask teachers to consider how children might think about the problem, and provide context appropriate for the specific video clip. When available, written work may be shown to teachers before viewing the video so that they might anticipate the child's thinking.

3. **View and discuss the video.**
   - First ask teachers to describe the video, that is, discuss what they saw without interpreting or evaluating what they see.
   - Teachers might then compare what they saw to what they expected, and also compare the child's reasoning to their own reasoning when they solved the problem.
   - Consider other implications for mathematics, teaching, and learning (e.g., the interviewer's or teacher's role, what a teacher would need to know to support the child, what follow-up problem might be posed next).

FIGURE 3.   A sequence for using video with teachers.

Step 1: Teachers Consider the Mathematics

The first step is for teachers to grapple with the mathematics themselves. We suggest asking teachers for two solutions to encourage them to start by solving the problem in a manner that is comfortable for them, whether it be procedurally or conceptually oriented. By honoring teachers' approaches, we model for them how important it is to start where the learner is. However, by asking for *two* approaches, we ask teachers to think outside their comfort zones and encourage them to consider other, often more conceptual, approaches.

Step 2: Teachers Consider Students' Thinking

The second step is for teachers to consider students' thinking as it relates to the problem. We suggest providing context appropriate for the specific video clip. For example, if the video shows a child using an invented or otherwise unconventional strategy, teachers might be asked to consider how a child might solve the problem *without* using the standard algorithm. If the video shows a student making a common error, teachers might be asked to predict the kinds of common errors one might see students make when solving this problem. Many of the video clips are accompanied by screen shots of written student work, and this work might be given to teachers before they view the video so that they might anticipate the child's thinking. A major teaching competency involves drawing inferences about students' understanding on the basis of looking at or grading students' written work.

Step 3: View and Discuss the Video

The third step is to view and discuss the video clip. Descriptions should be as objective as possible, and one test of a good description is that everyone can agree upon the description. For example, a description might read,

> *The child put up three fingers on her left hand and said, "Three," and then, when she put up additional fingers on her right hand, she counted, "Four, five, six, seven." The teacher asked the child what the answer was, and the child repeated the steps.*

We have found that people have a tendency to "climb the inference ladder" quickly. For example, the video clip described above might also be described as follows. (Notice that this description includes more inferences and evaluations than the first description.)

> *The child used her fingers to count to seven. That was really good. The teacher then asked for the answer, and the child must have thought the teacher was asking her to repeat what she did, so she explained her solution again. I think the child understood, but maybe the child did not realize that the last number she said, "seven," was the answer.*

After describing the solution, the teachers might then compare the child's thinking with the thinking they used to solve the problem. This discussion might highlight how differently students approach problems from the way teachers think. The teachers might also compare what the child in the video did with that which the teachers predicted. One advantage of asking teachers to make predictions is that by taking a stand on what they think might happen, they are more aware of ways in which they might have been surprised by what the child was thinking. Finally, many implications for mathematics, teaching, and learning might be raised by considering video. One particularly probing, but difficult, question for teachers is to consider "What next question might you pose to the student, and what are you hoping to learn or accomplish by using that question?"

Finding and Using Video Clips

General Content Information

The video clips have been categorized into clips about place value and whole number (Video Clips 100–207), clips about rational number (Video Clips 300–388), clips showing group work, whole-class work, or teacher reflection (Video Clips 500–526), and clips selected to illustrate interviewing techniques or challenges (Video Clips 600–607).

Using the Search Functionality

After inserting the DVD and allowing it to load the welcome page on your computer, click the button to begin. On the Videos tab, you will see two search options at the top and the Complete List of Clips through which you may scroll.

Search Option 1: By IMAP Categories and Terms

When you select a category in the left column, the terms that can be searched within that category populate the Terms window (just to the right of the Categories window). Then you may click on a number of Terms to populate the Your Search Criteria window at right. You may continue clicking on categories and terms until all the criteria you wish to include in one search populate Your Search Criteria. Notice that the Complete List of Clips below the search criteria dynamically updates with every term added and will state, "Showing X of 232 clips."

Search Terms

In the Glossary, located within the *Resources* tab and reproduced in Appendix A of this guide, each search term is defined according to the way we used the term in categorizing these video clips. Table 1 shows a list of the Search Categories and the Search Terms within each category.

TABLE 1.   Categories and Search Terms

Category	Search Terms		
Student gender	M F		
Student grade	K, 1st, 2nd, 3rd, 4th, 5th, 6th, Adult/PST		
Student ethnicity	African American Asian American Caucasian Latino Multi		
Content	Algebra Comparison Counting Decimal addition Decimal subtraction Decimals Equal sharing Fraction addition	Fraction division Fraction multiplication Fraction subtraction Fractions Identifying fractions Missing addend Money Place value	Renaming fractions Role of the unit Story problem Whole number addition Whole number division Whole number multiplication Whole number subtraction
Strategy	Composing/ decomposing numbers Counting back Counting on Counting up Derived fact Direct modeling Distributive property Drawing	Expanded algorithm Fingers Hundred chart Invented strategy Manipulatives Misconception Misconstrued strategy Number sense	Number sense not evident Patterns Procedure Recall Repeated addition Skip counting Standard algorithm
Teaching/ interviewing	Clarify Conceptual instruction Difficult interview Extension question In/out of context	Introducing interview Novice interviewer Probing Procedural instruction Scaffolding	Small group Student discourse Wait time Whole class
Miscellaneous	Cognitive dissonance Exceptional reasoning Intermediate	Language issue Primary Self-corrects	Spanish speaker Teacher reflection/advice Wrong answer

Refining Your Search or Beginning a New Search

- If you wish to refine your search, you may click on the red X next to Categories populating Your Search Criteria to eliminate all the Terms in that Category from your search. The Category will disappear from Your Search Criteria, and the clips showing below will dynamically update.

- If you have selected multiple terms from one category and wish to eliminate only one term from Your Search Criteria, click on that category in the left Category column to see the terms that you selected highlighted yellow in the Terms column.

Click on the one or two or more terms in the Terms column that you wish to eliminate from Your Search Criteria. The yellow highlighting will disappear, the term will disappear from Your Search Criteria, and the list of clips below will be dynamically updated.

- You may click on Categories and Terms to add additional categories and terms to Your Search Criteria at any time, and the list of clips below will update and display the new number of clips matching those criteria.

- If you wish to start a fresh search, you may click on the red X next to all categories populating Your Search Criteria until the entire column is blank. The heading above the clips will update to say "Complete List of Clips: Showing 232 of 232."

Search Results

For each clip, the listing includes a thumbnail picturing the child or adult in the clip, the clip number, and the title; Terms used to categorize the clip; the time length of the clip; Play Now button; Download menu; and Show Clip Info link. Some clips also display Related Clips with hotlinked clip numbers, View Screen Capture link, or both.

The clips in the search results will be those in the intersection of the Category terms. Within a category, the clips in the results will be those meeting the criteria in the union of the Search Terms. An example follows:

Category	Search Term	Results
Ethnicity	African American Asian American	All clips showing either African American students in Grades 1–3 working with place-value ideas or Asian American students in Grades 1–3 working with place-value ideas are included in the Search Results.
Grade	1st, 2nd, 3rd	That is, each clip has one of the selected attributes from each category chosen for searching. The Search Results show 3 matches for clips meeting these criteria.
Content	Place value	

Of course, by selecting fewer search terms, and thus conducting a less restrictive search, you increase the likelihood that clips with the selected attributes will be found among the 232 clips. The following sample searches have been designed to illustrate the effects of restricting searches to varying degrees:

Search #1

My criteria are too restrictive. No clips in the collection meet all these criteria, or the search criteria are not ones that occur together in our clips.

Category	Search Term	Results
Grade	1st, 2nd	**Showing 0 of 232**
Content	Fraction division	Although we have 64 clips of 1st and 2nd graders working on story problems, we have no clips of children in those grades working on fraction division.

Search #2

My criteria are insufficiently restrictive. My criteria of children in Grades 2–5 working on fractions matched 88 clips; this may be too many to be useful.

Category	Search Term	Results
Grade	2nd, 3rd, 4th, 5th	**Showing 88 of 232**
Content	Fractions	I could narrow my results by choosing fewer grade levels or by choosing the content more precisely (e.g., by choosing the *role of the unit* as the Search Term for the Content category).

Search #3

By further restricting my #2 search, I can more precisely meet my needs, and the search yields a reasonable number of clip choices.

Category	Search Term	Results
Grade	2nd, 3rd, 4th, 5th	**13 of 232 Clips Showing**
Content	Role of the unit	I could have narrowed my results by choosing fewer grade levels; however, I instead chose the content more precisely because the role of the unit is my primary interest in this search. By choosing the *role of the unit* as the Term for the Content category, I narrowed the results to 13 clips matching my criteria.

Search Option 2: By Child Name and Clip Number

Alternatively, on the right side of the screen at the top of the Videos tab, you may simply type a child's name or a specific clip number into the box and click the Search button to identify all the clips showing one child or the specific clip number you wish to retrieve. The Complete List of Clips below the search criteria updates to reflect your search option; it will indicate how many clips fit the criteria with "Showing X of 232 clips."

To return to viewing all 232 clips, click the Reset button below the Search button. To begin a fresh search for another clip number or child's name, simply type the new clip number or child name in the search box and click the Search button. Results will be updated below to reflect your new selection.

Using the Clips Identified in the Search Results

When you are presented with the list of video clips satisfying your search requirements, you may click on the Play Now button to view any of the clips in your search results. You also have the option to click on the Download menu and Show Clip Info link. Some clips also display Related Clips with hotlinked clip numbers, a View Screen Capture link, or both.

Play Now

Clicking the Play Now button will bring up the video with the clip number and title at top in the blue bar and the Transcript and Related Info in boxes to the right. At the bottom of the video player are buttons to pause the video, adjust the volume, show captions, and enlarge the video to full screen. You will be unable to view the transcript and related info in full screen mode, but you can always reclick the Full Screen button at the bottom to return to the smaller video window that includes the Transcript and Related Info boxes. The elapsed time and total time length of the video appear next to the video-play bar.

If you find transcripts or related info distracting, you may click the buttons Hide Transcript or Hide Related Info to eliminate this content; the buttons change to Show Transcript and Show Related Info in case you wish to view either. Related Info includes clip number and title, all the terms associated with the clip, Clip Info, and link to Download Menu.

Download

Clicking on this link to the right of the Play Now button displays a menu of two or three downloadable items.

Problem File.   Each video clip is accompanied by a Word document (called Problem File in the Download menu) containing the problem posed in the video and Video Preparation and Discussion Questions. At times, these Problem Files include notes referencing other video clips. When they do, hot-linked Related Clips are included with the corresponding video results. These Problem Files documents were designed to support facilitators in helping teachers consider the mathematics and children's thinking about the mathematics.

Transcript.   You may also download complete transcripts (select Transcript in the Download menu) for each clip. Facilitators may select transcript portions for analysis by teachers as part of their courses or workshops.

Screen Capture.   Additionally, many clips have associated jpeg files containing one screen capture (select Screen Capture in the Download menu) from the video clip; these still shots were created to support discussion and presentations.

Show Clip Info

Clicking on this link to the right of the Play Now button displays detailed information about the clip contents including background information, commentary on the clip, questions to consider, and often times the numbers of other clips in which the same child appears.

View Screen Capture

Clicking on this link to the right of the Play Now button displays the Screen Capture that is also available on the Download menu. The link allows you to preview the Screen Capture before deciding to download the JPEG file.

Related Clips

Some clip results display Related Clips with hotlinked clip numbers beneath the list of Terms. When the Video Preparation and Discussion section of the Problem File for the clip include suggestions that teachers view or compare additional clips, these links are provided for easy access to those related clips.

Resources Listed on the Resource Tab

Choose the Resources tab to view a number of resources in simple text or to download them as Word or PDF files. To access these resources from within the program, click on the desired resource. Its title will be highlighted in yellow, and the file will appear in the window to the right of the resource list.

- The Glossary shows definitions for the key words as we use them. In this document, we explain how we used the various search terms related to each search category (which appears in parentheses after the search term) in categorizing the clips in this collection. The Glossary contains our definitions for each of the search terms; we do not claim that the definitions we chose are standard definitions; they reflect our use of the terms. For example, "role of the unit" (content) is used as a descriptor for clips in which keeping track of the whole is important in the fraction problem posed. See Appendix A for the Glossary.

- References appear among the resources. These references and other references cited in this guide appear in the References section at the end of this guide.

This product includes several resources related to interviewing, including the following Instructor Interview Guide. The separate interview-related resources are in bold and are described within this document.

Appendix
Instructor Interview Guide

Introduction

When our students conduct interviews of children as part of their mathematics course or their course on teaching and learning, they report that these experiences are among the most memorable and important of the course. This document is provided to support instructors who would like to assign their students to conduct a child interview.

We recognize that many instructors have experience with constructing and carrying out interviews. This document gives an example of the process from our experience. We recognize that student interviews can be organized and carried out in many ways, and the details we provide below are intended to be viewed only as *a* way, not *the* way.

Purpose for the Interview

Our goal for these interviews is for prospective elementary school teachers to learn as much as they can about children's mathematical thinking and understanding. Most preservice and in-service teachers are surprised by what they learn when they listen carefully to children. Sometimes children know more than was expected; sometimes they know less. Always the interviews are interesting.

When working with children, most prospective elementary school teachers are initially oriented toward *teaching* the child, and they often attempt to teach by helping the child attain correct answers. Doing so is natural because prospective elementary school teachers care about children and want to help them. However, we discourage this sort of teaching during the interviews, because once our students begin to teach, their focus shifts from understanding the child's mathematical thinking to considering ways they might explain something to the child. In other words, the focus shifts from the child to the adult. Although for prospective teachers to focus on issues of teaching is important, we think that our students must first develop some understanding of the children they will be teaching.

Preparation for the Interview

The first interview our students conduct is on early number. Examples below are drawn from this context.

We attempt to prepare our students for their first interview in the following way:

1. We provide students with a set of questions and tasks.

   Among the Resources are sample interview questions and tasks. We have found that even graduate students and practicing teachers have difficulty constructing interview questions that focus on assessing children's understanding of the underlying conceptual ideas, so we provide students with questions.

2. We discuss the relative difficulties of the problems, some strategies students commonly use to solve these problems, and some ways children think about the problems. (Story 6: Interviewing includes some such information.)

   Video Clip #607 shows a child responding to several story problems from the Early Number interview. We ask students to attend to which problems the child could solve, which he could not, and how he solved various problems. He correctly answered the multiplication problem but struggled with some addition and subtraction problems.

3. We have our students think about how to begin an interview and how to set the child at ease at the outset.

   Video Clips #602 and #604 are of two interviewers introducing their interviews to the children to be interviewed. Notice how they each attempt to set the child at ease, how they explain to the child that he may solve problems however he would like, and that he will be asked to explain his thinking. The interviewers also explain that some problems will be difficult and others will be easy, and so the children should not be concerned if they are unable to answer all the questions correctly.

4. We help our students consider issues that might arise during an interview.

   For example, we raise the issue of wait time in discussing Video Clip #607 and issues of scaffolding and posing follow-up questions in discussing Video Clip #601.

5. We discuss the **Interview Write-Up** that the students will submit.

   We include a copy of our interview write-up assignment in the Resources. Note that we refer to a partner in the assignment. Because of circumstances available to us, we teach some courses on site at local elementary schools, and we often interview children drawn from classes there. We place our prospective elementary school teachers in pairs when they interview one child; one student leads the interview while the other student takes notes and interjects on occasion. We often loan the students tape recorders to audiotape the interview to allow for deeper reflection on the interview. If your students arrange and conduct their interviews on their own time and work alone, we recommend that they audiotape the interviews.

Following are some observations we have made that might be useful to you when teachers or teacher candidates plan their interviews.

- Some prospective elementary school teachers do not know how to prepare for an interview. These students benefit from explicit support you provide. For example, in addition to assigning our students to view video clips of interviews for homework in preparation for their interviews, we watch video clips in class and stop the video and ask students to consider what the child understands. We also ask them to suggest what they might do next if they were interviewing. We also have role played: Either the instructor plays the role of the child while the class interviews, or the students meet in groups to play the roles of the child and the interviewer.

- For homework preceding the interview, we give the students copies of the interview questions and often ask them to predict whether and how a child will answer some of the questions. At the least, the students are then familiar with the interview questions.

- We construct with the students an interview-materials checklist, including the interview questions, paper for the children to use and for the interviewers to take notes, an extra pen or pencil, appropriate manipulatives or counters, and a tape recorder and tape.

Our Interview Sequence

Early-Number Interview

We use the **Early-Number Interview** with children in Grades 1 and 2. We also include some common interview situations (**Primary What-Ifs**) for discussion or role playing in preparing for the interview. The file provides a set of possible responses to common reactions young children have when asked so solve early-number problems.

Place-Value Interviews

Our students conduct two interviews with third graders: In **Place-Value Interview 1** they learn about the child's place-value understanding; they pursue some ideas in greater depth in **Place-Value Interview 2**.

Rational-Number Interviews

Our students conduct several interviews on rational number. Each student pair works with the same fifth grader for all interviews on rational numbers. They first use the **Fraction Assessment** to find out how the child thinks about fractions. They often use equal-sharing (Empson, 1995; Empson & Levi, in press) tasks, which we have found to be excellent tasks for raising multiple-representations (Clement, 2004; Lesh, Post, & Behr, 1987) issues about partitioning, equal-sized pieces, naming fractions, and equivalence. However, even a small number of tasks may be time consuming when the interviewer directs the child toward these many issues. Interviews could be constructed from tasks in the **Equal-Sharing Tasks 1 and 2** documents.

Gretchen's Story

Video Clip #155 shows a child, Gretchen, who uses the standard algorithm incorrectly to solve 70 – 23. She then solves the problem correctly in two ways, using tools. However, at the end of the interview, she believes that her algorithmic solution is the correct one. The interviewer ends the interview by saying that the problem is just something she will need to continue to consider. In Gretchen's Story, the interviewer describes her conversation with Gretchen a few days after the interview took place. In this conversation the confusion is resolved.

PART III

Thematic Stories

Introduction to Stories

Fundamentally people enjoy stories, but stories are also important as a source for learning about others and the world. Thus, stories are powerful. Great literature is enduring; it captures aspects of the human condition that have been issues throughout time. Specific contexts may change, but the issues endure. In a sense, each of these video clips can be thought of as providing a story, and although we do not suggest that each story is representative of all students, taken as a whole, the video clips capture significant examples of students' mathematical activity in schools.

Although these video clips might be used individually to demonstrate a particular mathematical or pedagogical point, when you become familiar with the clips and begin to select your personal favorites, you may find that by combining several clips, you can tell a richer story. Of the many stories that have emerged for us from these video clips, we have selected six to share with you. Five of these stories capture principles about mathematics teaching and learning that we have found to be important for our work with prospective and practicing teachers. The sixth story, about interviewing, is different from the other stories because its focus is skill-based as opposed to principle-based. These six stories are certainly not the only ones we could tell, and we expect that when you learn about these video clips, you will choose other stories to tell. Our six stories are listed below.

> **Story 1:** Students' Answers Are Only Part of the Story
>
> **Story 2:** Understanding Is Not an All or Nothing Enterprise (one appendix)
>
> **Story 3:** Procedural and Conceptual Understanding
>
> **Story 4:** Developing Fraction Understanding (two appendices)
>
> **Story 5:** Mathematical Proficiency
>
> **Story 6:** Introduction to Interviewing

Story Length

We generally estimate that each story might be shared in one 3-hour session. However, we recognize that the amount of time required for a story will vary widely, on the bases of the facilitator's goals, the audience, and the circumstances. For example, earlier we described a sequence for using video whereby before viewing and discussing a video clip, teachers consider the mathematics and they consider students' thinking about the mathematics. If either, or both, of these steps are omitted, then the stories will be shortened. Furthermore, a shorter version could be constructed by omitting some of the video clips. Ultimately, however, if you are working with a particularly reflective group of teachers or if you set out to include more analysis of the mathematics or pedagogical issues, these stories could easily last 5 hours, 10 hours, or longer.

Using a Story

Each story contains background information and analysis for the facilitator, and specific suggestions for video clips to use and questions to pose before and after showing the video to teachers. The stories are written in a prescriptive manner, that is, we are explicit about what a facilitator might do and say, but we recognize that facilitators will use these materials in ways that make sense to them, and we do not mean to imply that our suggestions are the only way to share each story.

In each story, questions designed to be posed to teachers, by facilitators, are set in boxes.

STORY 1
Students' Answers Are Only Part of the Story

Correct answers have always been taken as a measure of understanding, rightfully so. Students who score 750 on the mathematics SAT exam generally have a deeper mathematical understanding of the content assessed than students who score 450; or students who score in the 99th percentile on a district standardized test generally understand more than students who score in the 40th percentile. However, as important as students' learning to answer correctly is, the fundamental goal of teaching mathematics is to help students become more mathematically proficient by developing richer, more connected ways of understanding. Furthermore, when getting correct answers becomes the goal of instruction, students often find shortcuts whereby they can memorize a procedure for arriving at an answer without grappling with the underlying conceptual ideas. From years of working with individual students, we have found that students often arrive at correct answers without having the associated understanding one might assume accompanies the right answer; that is, students often obtain right answers for the wrong reasons. We have also found that a student may get a wrong answer but have a valid way of reasoning. The purpose of Story 1 is to illustrate that answers are only part of the story.

STORY 1, Outline

Part I. Correct answers are often associated with valid, rich reasoning.
(2 video clips)

Part II. Correct answers are often *not* associated with valid reasoning.
(3 video clips)

Part III. Incorrect answers are often associated with valid reasoning.
(2 video clips)

STORY 1, Part I

Correct answers are often associated with valid, rich reasoning.

In the first part of this story, we illustrate that students may reason in rich ways and arrive at correct answers. Many video clips highlight this point, and we note two, one at a primary grade (Arriel, Video Clip #119, Grade 2, 1:53) and another at an intermediate grade (Felisha, Video Clip #325, Grade 4, 3:10). This first point is *not* difficult to make because most people believe that correct answers reflect valid reasoning. However, by seeing a few such video clips, teachers will have examples of how students look who have rich understanding of the task. Furthermore, the teachers may use these clips as contrasts to video clips of students in Parts II and III of the story.

STORY 1, Part I, Clip 1

Before Viewing Video Clip #119 (Arriel, Grade 2, 1:53)

> You are about to watch a second grader, Arriel, consider the following problem:
>
> *Suppose that you had some toy cars, and you went to the store and bought four more toy cars. Suppose that then you had nine toy cars altogether. How many toy cars did you have to start with?*
>
> What kind of problem is this for an adult? What kind of problem is it for a 6-year-old child? How might a child solve the problem?

Analysis.   Although many adults think of this as a subtraction problem because the answer, 5, is the result of subtracting 4 from 9, research has shown that younger students tend not to view this problem as subtraction because the context is about obtaining more cars. The CGI researchers referred to this problem as a *join, start unknown,* to reflect the joining action in the context and the fact that the missing quantity is at the start of the problem, before any action takes place. If one represented this problem using a number sentence, one might use ___ + 4 = 9. Because younger children often attempt to solve problems by modeling the problem using counters, this problem is more difficult to solve than one in which the result is unknown (e.g., 5 + 4 = ___) or the change is unknown (e.g., 5 + __ = 9).

After Viewing Video Clip #119 (Arriel, Grade 2, 1:53)

> Describe what you saw in the video. Try to separate a description of what you observed from your interpretation/evaluation of the child's or interviewer's behaviors or intentions.

(Note that the purpose for separating the description from the interpretations/evaluations is so that teachers learn to separate what they explicitly see in the video from the voices in their heads containing the *should*s and *ought to*s.)

Description.   Of course, the clip could be described in many ways. Here is one way. While solving the problem, Arriel made a train of 9 cubes, but determining whether she already knew the answer at that time is difficult. When she explained that she already knew that $5 + 4 = 9$, the interviewer asked why she had used the blocks. Arriel explained that she needed the blocks to check her answer. Note that Arriel remembered the problem and was able to restate it in her own words, including the quantities, not just the numbers.

Interpretation/Evaluation.   Arriel solved the problem correctly and she seemed to understand the context. She also seemed to have memorized the number fact $5 + 4 = 9$. Perhaps she was taught number families in school. When the interviewer asked, "So, did you need to use the cubes for this," she may have meant for the word *need* to imply that Arriel needed the cubes to solve the problem, whereas Arriel seemed to used the word *need* to refer to what was necessary to show why her answer was correct.

STORY 1, Part I, Clip 2

Before Viewing Video Clip #325 (Felisha, End of Grade 4, 3:10)

> You are about to watch a student, Felisha, at the end of fourth grade, think about the following problem. Please solve it.
>
> *You and three friends are having a math party and you want to evenly share an award-winning cookie. You cut the cookie into 4 equal pieces. However, before you eat it, one of your friends gets a call and leaves without taking any cookie. You and your two friends decide that you want to eat all of the cookie, but you each want the same amount. How might you cut up the cookie, given that it is already cut into 4 equal pieces?*
>
> *How much cookie would you each get?*

Discuss solutions to this problem. Did any of the teachers give an answer using fraction language? If so, how did they reason about the problem?

After Viewing Video Clip #325 (Felisha, End of Grade 4, 3:10)

> Describe what you saw in the video.
>
> Explain Felisha's reasoning.
>
> What do you think about Felisha's reasoning?

Analysis.   Felisha drew four students and one cookie; she partitioned the cookie into four equal pieces, and she "handed out" one piece of the cookie to each student. Her answer, "one fourth," indicates that she was reasoning flexibly among the real-life context (4 children sharing a cookie), the diagram she created, and the language of fractions (that each of those pieces is one fourth). When told that one child left, Felisha crossed off one of the children, presumably to reflect that only three children remained. She re-partitioned one piece of cookie, and distributed a small piece to each of the three remaining children. When asked to explain how much each person got, she said that each received one fourth and one twelfth. Note the slight hesitation before she named the "one twelfth," presumably because she was thinking about how much of the whole each of those smaller partitions represented. Also, note that Felisha stated that, added together, the two pieces represented one third. The interviewer asked Felisha to represent this symbolically, which she did correctly, writing 1/4 + 1/12 = 1/3. The interviewer wondered how Felisha reasoned to determine that 1/4 + 1/12 equals 1/3, but Felisha's answer does not leave us feeling confident that we know how she reasoned. We conjecture that Felisha connected the fact that each child received 1/4 + 1/12 with the fact that, when a whole is shared evenly among three people, regardless of how the whole is partitioned, each child receives 1/3. But this is only a conjecture. However Felisha reasoned, we take this video clip as a second example that correct answers are often associated with valid, rich reasoning.

STORY 1, Part II

Correct answers are often *not* associated with valid reasoning.

This second part of the story highlights the need for teachers to "dig below the surface" of correct answers to determine whether the correct answers are associated with the kind of rich reasoning we value. Often students have no valid mathematical reasoning underlying their correct answers. We have chosen three video clips to make this point. The first two are similar in that the students answered correctly but clearly were confused about the procedures they used (Video Clip #388 and Video Clip #363); the third video clip differs from the first two in that the child clearly had mastered the procedure but did not seem to have access to the underlying conceptual understanding (Video Clip #156, Hally, Grade 3, 2:27).

STORY 1, Part II, Clip 1

Before Viewing Video Clip #388 (Megan & Donna, Grade 5, 1:53)

Find two different ways to compare 4.7 and 4.70.

How might fifth-grade students reason about this?

Analysis. This video clip shows two students, Megan and Donna, correctly comparing 4.7 and 4.70. However, as will be seen, they did not understand the procedure they were applying, nor did they understand decimals. We suggest you do not mention to your teachers anything about Megan's and Donna's confusion before viewing the video clip because the teachers' first impression may be that the students had understanding about decimals, and this first impression is important for the story. Depending on the work you are doing with your prospective or practicing teachers, you might spend time working through how students make meaning for decimals.

Note that this video clip will be shown in two sections. The first section is only the first 21 seconds.

After Viewing 0:00–0:21 of Video Clip #388 (Megan & Donna, Grade 5)

> What might you conclude now about the reasoning of the students?

Analysis. On the basis of only the first 21 seconds of the video clip, one might assume that Megan and Donna understood decimals.

After Viewing 0:22–0:46 of Video Clip #388 (Megan & Donna, Grade 5)

> What might you conclude now about the reasoning of the students?

Analysis. These two students seemed to be comparing decimals by appending zeros so that the numbers have the same number of digits to the right of the decimal point. This procedure, which is often taught in schools, results in correct answers, but students often do not understand why appending the zeros is mathematically permissible. Furthermore, this procedure enables students to get the right answer without understanding decimal numbers. Although one need not watch the entire video clip, viewing the rest of the clip provides additional evidence in support of the conclusion that these students did not understand decimals.

STORY 1, Part II, Clip 2

The next video clip is similar to the previous clip in that a student, also a fifth grader, gets the right answer for the wrong reason. If you show this clip immediately after viewing Clip #388, we think that the video clip might be shown in its entirety, without stopping after Melissa answered correctly. However, if you use this clip without using Clip #388, we suggest that you stop the video clip after Melissa gives the correct answer and ask the teachers what they conclude about her understanding.

Before Viewing Video Clip #363 (Melissa, Grade 5, 0:54)

> You are about to observe another student, also a fifth grader, who, like the two girls in the previous video clip, answered correctly for the wrong reason. Melissa compared 5/3 and 1-2/3. How might she have used invalid reasoning to correctly conclude that these two fractions are equal?

After Viewing Video Clip #363 (Melissa, Grade 5, 0:54)

> What might you conclude about Melissa's understanding of fractions?

Analysis.   This video clip is baffling to us. One explanation is that Melissa was explaining an incorrect approach she used when working with fractions. Another explanation is that Melissa first concluded that the fractions were equal and then devised a justification to support her conclusion. Or perhaps the teachers with whom you are working will provide another explanation. Whatever the case, we conclude that this video clip provides additional evidence for the principle that correct answers are not necessarily associated with valid reasoning.

STORY 1, Part II, Clip 3

We selected the next video clip to again demonstrate the principle that correct answers are not necessarily associated with valid reasoning, but this clip is different from the first two. Hally, a third grader, quickly and efficiently subtracted $1000 - 6$, and then $1000 - 1$, using the standard multidigit-subtraction algorithm. Teachers may observe that Hally, when asked for another approach, did not see that $1000 - 1$ might be solved without applying an algorithm.

Before Viewing Video Clip #156 (Hally, Grade 3, 2:27)

> Solve $1000 - 1$ two different ways.
>
> Describe what mathematical understanding is associated with each of the two approaches you chose for subtracting $1000 - 1$.
>
> Do you have a preference for which approach you would like third graders to use to solve $1000 - 1$? Why?

After Viewing Video Clip #156 (Hally, Grade 3, 2:27)

> Describe Hally's solution.
>
> What understanding of place value can you infer from Hally's solution?

Analysis.   Hally efficiently applied the standard multidigit-subtraction algorithm. However, when asked whether she could solve this problem another way, she could not think of another approach. Furthermore, when she used the multidigit-addition algorithm, her thinking seemed to be focused around the calculational meaning of the regrouped 1s. That is, although each 1 represents a different amount, all are treated as

1s in the algorithm, and that seemed to be the only way that Hally thought about them. Hally's clip is different from the previous two clips, because there is nothing incorrect about her reasoning. Instead, this video clip provides an example of a student who likely would test well, but on deeper reflection, seems to be missing the conceptual foundation for the procedure she has learned to efficiently apply.

STORY 1, Part III

Incorrect answers are often associated with valid reasoning.

In Part II of this story, we provided examples of students who answered correctly even though they did not seem to understand; Part III shows students who *do* understand but who arrived at incorrect answers. This part includes two video clips, both from primary grades, one of a boy (Video Clip #131, Conner, Grade 1, 2:59) and the other of a girl (Video Clip #186, Nicole, Grade 2, 1:15); both children initially answered incorrectly but showed evidence that they understood the concepts the interviewer was assessing. The evidence that the boy understood place value is clear from his explanation of his incorrect answer, whereas the evidence for the girl's understanding is provided only after the interviewer posed a follow-up question that she considered.

STORY 1, Part III, Clip 1

Before Viewing 0:00–0:55 of Video Clip #131 (Conner, Grade 1, 2:59)

> You are about to watch a first grader, Conner, consider the following problem:
>
> *Connor had 39 baseball cards. His grandfather gave him 25 more baseball cards. How many baseball cards does he have now?*
>
> How might a child solve this problem without using a standard algorithm?

Analysis.   Conner used his knowledge of place value to solve this problem.

After Viewing 0:00–0:55 of Video Clip #131 (Conner, Grade 1, 2:59)

> Describe Connor's thinking.
>
> What did you learn about Connor's understanding?

Analysis.   Conner's answer of 61 is incorrect, but his reasoning showed that Conner had flexible understanding of tens and ones. He seemed to have correctly answered a different problem, 39 + 22, but, more important, he explained that he added 20 (from the 22) to the 39, to get 59, and then he added 2 more to get 61. If the interviewer's objective was to determine whether Connor would give the correct answer, then we learned that he did not. If her objective was to determine whether Connor understood place value sufficiently to apply his understanding to a multidigit-addition problem, then we learned that he did. If you decide to watch the rest of the video clip, you will see that Connor realized that he had solved a different problem from that which had been posed, and he then correctly solved 39 + 25. However, for purposes of this story, we suggest that the point is made clearly from watching just the first 55 seconds of the video clip.

STORY 1, Part III, Clip 2

Before Viewing Video Clip #186 (Nicole, Grade 2, 1:15)

> You are about to watch a second grader, Nicole, early in the academic year, consider the following problem.
>
> *Twenty children are going on a field trip to McDonald's. Parents are going to help drive, but each car only has four seat belts for children. How many cars would we need to drive all 20 children to McDonald's?*
>
> Nicole had not yet learned about division in school. How might she think about this problem?

Analysis. Most primary-grades students have yet to learn formally about division and probably have not seen the division symbol. However, they know about sharing equally, and, if provided counters, they are often able to model whole-number multiplication and division situations that are placed in relevant contexts.

Nicole was interviewed in front of a group of 30 prospective elementary school teachers enrolled in a mathematics methodology class. Many people are concerned, sometimes even horrified, by the idea of interviewing a child in front of a group of people, but Nicole appeared to be quite relaxed. In fact, we would argue that during this interview, Nicole was the most relaxed person in the room! The interviewer was working hard to think about what questions to pose next while listening carefully to Nicole, and the prospective teachers were imagining how upset they would be if they were to be interviewed in front of a group of people about their mathematical understanding.

After Viewing Video Clip #186 (Nicole, Grade 2, 1:15)

> Describe what you saw.
>
> What did you learn about Nicole's understanding?

Analysis. Nicole used the cubes, made two rows of 4, and answered, incorrectly, "Eight." At this point, we do not know how she was reasoning. The interviewer asked if she could show the 20 children, a question that provided scaffolding support to the child. We find noteworthy that Nicole counted out 20, placing them in groups of 4, and was able to conclude that they would need 5 cars. Although we would not conclude from this video clip that Nicole completely understood how to solve whole-number division problems, we think that the entire video clip provides evidence that she understood the context and was able to distinguish among the three quantities in the problem: the total number of children, the number of children in each car, and the number of cars. The initial incorrect answer was not a good indication of Nicole's understanding.

STORY 2
Understanding Is Not an All or Nothing Enterprise

People hold beliefs about learning and teaching, and the beliefs one holds affect one's approach toward learning and teaching. One belief that we think people tend to hold is that one either understands something or does not. For example, people generally think that if we pose a question and a student answers incorrectly, then the student does not understand, whereas if another student answers correctly, then the second student understands. However, we have found that this over-simplified view of understanding is generally wrong. Instead, we have found that most people understand something about nearly everything (age appropriate) and few or none understand everything about anything. Instead of thinking that a child who answers incorrectly simply does not understand, teachers who develop more nuanced views began to consider instead what the child *does* understand so that they could build on that partial understanding. Further, on seeing evidence of understanding on the part of a student, instead of considering that the understanding is complete, they consider how they might extend the student's thinking on the basis of what the student seems to understand. In this story, we use video clips to illustrate these ideas by considering students' informal, though incomplete, understandings.

STORY 2, Outline

Part I. Children can solve problems before being taught how to solve them. (3 video clips)

Part II. Although students can use their informal knowledge to solve problems, their informal knowledge is disconnected from the formalisms they have been taught. (2 video clips, the first in three parts and the second in two parts)

Part III. Even deep understanding of a concept may be incomplete. Understanding can be extended. (1 video clip in two parts)

STORY 2, Part I

Children can solve problems before being taught how to solve them.

Teachers who begin to offer young children opportunities to solve problems they have not yet been taught to solve are often surprised by the strategies the children devise. Before learning number facts and algorithms adults would use, children can solve story problems by modeling, drawing, counting, and adapting facts they know. Among the many primary-grade examples, consider the young children who solve division problems using their informal understanding of sharing and removing groups. These children are not exceptional. Research has shown that at the end of the school year, 70% of kindergartners were successful in solving such problems (Carpenter, Ansell, Franke, Fennema, & Weisbeck, 1993). To illustrate this use of informal knowledge, consider two first graders' solutions to division problems: One uses a dealing strategy (Cheyenne, Clip #127, Grade 1, 1:34) and another (Connor, Clip #129, Grade 1, 1:20) uses skip counting.

In an intermediate-grade example of use of informal knowledge, a child relies on her understanding of the clock to complete a multidigit-multiplication problem (Brooke, Clip #124, Grade 5, 1:37). Many teachers appreciate the sophistication of the informal reasoning with which children come to school. However, a brief anecdote highlights that novice teachers may not appreciate students' informal, preinstructional knowledge. A group of prospective teachers enrolled in a credential program once conducted interviews of kindergartners early in the school year. During the post-interview discussion, the prospective teachers marveled at how much more the students knew than the prospective teachers had expected. One prospective teacher commented that the teacher had taught a great deal in just a few weeks. In other words, for this prospective teacher, anything the students knew about mathematics must have been taught in school!

Although the examples of rich reasoning on the part of children are many at the primary grades, they seem to be more rare among older children, except among students who have been encouraged to think for themselves about how to solve problems instead of relying solely on memorized algorithms.

STORY 2, Part I, Clip 1

Before Viewing Video Clip #127 (Cheyenne, Grade 1, 1:34)

> You are about to watch a first grader, Cheyenne, consider the following problem:
>
> *There were 18 cupcakes at the party, and there were six children at the party. If we wanted to share the 18 cupcakes fairly, how many cupcakes would each child get?*
>
> What kind of problem is this for an adult? What kind of problem is this for a 6-year-old child? How might a young child solve the problem?

Analysis.   Although most people see this problem as division, to children it relates to a sharing situation that is familiar to them. Division problems generally have three quantities: the total, the number of groups, and the number per group. Because in this problem, called *partitive division* or *equal-sharing division,* the total number of cupcakes and the number of groups to be formed (the number of children sharing the cupcakes) are given, a common solution strategy is to deal out the cupcakes, one at a time to the three children in turn.

After Viewing Video Clip #127 (Cheyenne, Grade 1, 1:34)

> Describe what you saw in the video.
>
> Explain Cheyenne's reasoning.

Analysis.   For most children in the first grade in the United States, including the child in this video clip, the problems they have solved in mathematics that have involved two numbers have been solved either by adding or subtracting the numbers. In spite of this, the child did not simply add or subtract the two numbers in the problem. Instead, she made sense of the problem as one involving sharing equally 18 cupcakes among 6 children. Furthermore, she solved this problem even though she may not be familiar with the word *division* or with the symbol (÷) for division.

STORY 2, Part I, Clip 2

The second clip shows another first grader solving a division problem, but a problem that differs from the one Cheyenne solved.

Before Viewing Video Clip #129 (Connor, Grade 1, 1:20)

> You are about to watch a first grader, Connor, consider the following problem:
>
> *Twenty children are going on a field trip to the zoo in private cars. Each car can take only 4 children. How many cars do we need to take all 20 children to the zoo?*
>
> How might a young child solve the problem?

In this problem, called *quotitive, measurement,* or *repeated-subtraction* division, the total number of children going on the field trip and the number in each group (the number of children per car) are given.

After Viewing Video Clip #129 (Connor, Grade 1, 1:20)

> Describe what you saw in the video.
>
> Explain Connor's reasoning.
>
> Explain the interviewer's reaction to Connor's solution.

Analysis.   Connor was asked to find the number of groups to be formed (cars needed). A common strategy for solving this problem by modeling is to count 20 blocks, remove groups of 4 (repeatedly subtract), and determine the number of groups of 4 in 20. Connor's skip-counting solution is more sophisticated and more prone to error, but his reasoning is appropriate.

STORY 2, Part I, Clip 3

Before Viewing Video Clip #124, (Brooke, Grade 5, 1:37)

> You are about to watch Brooke, a fifth grader, think about the following problem. Please solve it without using a standard algorithm.
>
> *15 × 12*

Discuss solutions to this problem. What knowledge was assumed by the teachers?

After Viewing Video Clip #124, (Brooke, Grade 5, 1:37)

> Describe what you saw in the video.
>
> Explain Brooke's reasoning.
>
> How might you symbolize Brooke's solution? Consider what understandings Brooke shows in employing her strategy.
>
> Is Brooke's strategy generalizable? That is, might this solution be applied to all multiplication problems? If not, then to what numbers might it be applied?
>
> How could you help Brooke extend her understanding?

Analysis.   Brooke used her understanding of the clock to reason that for each 4 in 12 she had four 15s or 60, which she knew because of knowing that an hour has four 15-minute segments. She realized that she had three of these groups of four 15s. She added the three 60s mentally to determine her answer.

STORY 2, Part II

Although students can use their informal knowledge to solve problems, their informal knowledge is disconnected from the formalisms they have been taught.

This second part of the story about understanding illustrates that students have informal understanding on which they can draw to solve problems but that the connection of this informal knowledge to formalisms of mathematics may be missing. However, this informal knowledge provides a foundation on which teachers can build so that the formalisms may be developed meaningfully. We have chosen two video clips to make this point. In the first clip (Video Clip #148, Freddie, Grade 3, 6:15), a third grader misapplied a standard algorithm to solve a take-away-subtraction problem then correctly, using sense making, solved a missing-addend problem with the same numbers. He was next asked to solve 400 – 150 again, now without a context. Although he realized that his first effort was incorrect, in this solution he made a different error to get 300: He said that one cannot take something from nothing, cannot take 5 from 0, so 0 – 5 is 0, without considering regrouping from the 400. Finally he was asked to solve 400 – 150 using blocks, which he did correctly, explaining each step he used, including exchanging 1 flat (100) for 10 longs (of 10 each) so that he could subtract the 50 in 150. When asked which solution for 400 – 150 was correct, he stated that his last symbolic solution was the correct one. He did not relate his regrouping in his correctly modeled solution with possible regrouping in the symbolic situation—the formal and informal solutions were not yet related for Freddie. In the second clip, a fraction situation (Video Clip #341, Francisco, Grade 5, 3:51) a fifth grader was unable to subtract 4 – 1/8, presented symbolically. He used a drawing to answer 4 – 1/8 in a context of pizzas. To the surprise of the preservice teacher interviewing him, Francisco saw no relationship between the problems in and out of context. Like Freddie, Francisco had yet to make the connections between his informal and formal knowledge; for Francisco, the missing connections were between his informal knowledge of fractions and the formalism in subtracting fractions presented symbolically.

STORY 2, Part II, Clip 2

Clip 1 can be viewed in three parts: Part 1 shows Freddie applying a subtraction algorithm incorrectly to solve a take-away-subtraction problem. In Part 2, Freddie correctly solved a missing-addend problem with the same numbers used in Part 1. In Part 3, Freddie was asked to solve the same symbolic problem he solved in Part 1, which he did differently but still incorrectly, and then to model the problem with blocks, which he did correctly. He believed that his incorrect symbolic solution was the correct one.

Before Viewing Part 1 (0:00–0:52) of Video Clip #148, (Freddie, Grade 3, 6:15)

Freddie is asked to solve the following problem:

Carlo has 400 baseball cards in his collection. He sold 150 cards. How many cards does he have left?

How might he solve it?

Discuss possible solutions that Freddie might provide for the problem.

After viewing Part 1 (0:00–0:52) of Video Clip #148 (Freddie, Grade 3)

Describe Freddie's solution.

On the basis of this solution, what is your interpretation of Freddie's understanding of subtraction? Of his number sense?

How would you expect Freddie to approach the following problem using mental computation?

What if I had 150 seashells, and I went to the beach and collected some more. By the time I got done, I had 400 seashells. How many did I collect?

Analysis.   In Part 1 of this clip, Freddie made a common error (0 – 5 = 5) in attempting to subtract 400 – 150 symbolically, his choice of representation for the baseball-card problem, a separating situation in which the result is unknown. On the basis of the first 53 seconds of the video clip, one might assume that Freddie lacks understanding of subtraction and that his number sense is suspect. Discuss ways he might approach the new problem, a missing-addend problem or a joining situation in which the change is unknown, which he was asked to solve using mental computation. (Note that if you are working with a group learning to conduct interviews, you should consider stopping the video at 0:29, after Freddie gave his incorrect answer of 350 but before he explained his reasoning, and ask what participants think Freddie was thinking.)

After Viewing Part 2 (0:52–2:32) of Video Clip #148 (Freddie, Grade 3)

Describe Freddie's solution strategy for the second problem.

How did Freddie's solution to this problem reinforce or change your earlier view of Freddie's mathematical understanding, his number sense?

Do you expect Freddie to recognize now that his solution to the first problem was incorrect? Why or why not?

In the next segment, Freddie again applied a subtraction algorithm. His new answer is 300. Explain how Freddie might be thinking in answering this way.

Freddie was next asked to use blocks to solve 400 – 150. If he did so correctly, what effect would you expect his solution to have on his thinking about his algorithmic solutions?

Analysis.   In Part 2 of the clip, Freddie invoked number sense in adding on to the 150 to reach 400 and keeping track of the amounts he added. How he related his solution in this joining situation to finding the difference between the same numbers in the baseball-card take-away situation is unclear. When he was asked to again subtract symbolically, he said that his first symbolic subtraction was incorrect. However, in again approaching the problem symbolically, he decided that in the ten's place, 0 – 5 = 0 "because if you have zero and you take away 5—well, that's impossible, because you don't have any numbers. So I guess it would be zero." He was asked to use blocks to model and solve the problem, which he did correctly.

After Viewing Part 3 (2:32–6:15) of Video Clip #148 (Freddie, Grade 3)

> Describe Freddie's two solutions for 400 – 150.
>
> Does Freddie's choice of his symbolic solution as the correct solution surprise you? Why or why not?
>
> How might you respond next to Freddie?

Analysis.   In Part 3 of the clip, Freddie used blocks to model 400 – 150. He regrouped 1 flat (100) as 10 longs (10 each) and removed 5 of the 10 longs. His modeled solution was correct but at the end, he believed that his second symbolic solution was the correct solution instead of his blocks solution.

Note 1.   To show that Freddie is not unique in lacking a connection between his formal and informal solutions, see Video Clip #155 (Gretchen, Grade 1, 5:42) and Gretchen's Story in the Resources section of the Searchable IMAP Video Collection.

Note 2.   The disconnection between formal and informal mathematics may occur when a child immediately invokes the formalism, even when she could very easily solve the problem posed simply by thinking about it informally. For an example, see Video Clip #144 (Vanessa, Grade 3, 2:29), in which the child, after she was prompted to solve the problem mentally, said that the thinking solution was easier but that she used the algorithm because it was more challenging. We believe that solving the problem informally simply did not occur to the child because the focus in her mathematics class is most likely on mathematical formalisms. However, even Freddie, in whose class the children are invited to devise their own solutions, invoked the formalism before using any of the sense-making approaches with which he was clearly capable of solving the problems.

STORY 2, Part II, Clip 2

Clip 2 can be viewed in two parts. In this second clip (Video Clip #341, Francisco, Grade 5, 3:51), chosen to show the lack of connection students may have between their informal understanding and mathematical formalism, Francisco was asked to solve 4 – 1/8 and said that he could not solve it. The problem was then posed in the context of having 4 pizzas and eating 1/8 of one of the pizzas; Francisco drew pizzas to solve the problem with ease. He did not see a connection between the two problems, to the surprise of the novice interviewer.

**Before Viewing Part 1 (0:00–2:06) of Video Clip #341
(Francisco, Grade 5, 3:51)**

Francisco was asked to solve 4 − 1/8.

He correctly solved $4\frac{3}{8} - 2\frac{1}{8}$ symbolically. How do you expect him to solve 4 − 1/8?

Discuss possible solutions Francisco might provide.

**After Viewing Part 1 (0:00–2:06) of Video Clip #341
(Francisco, Grade 5, 3:51)**

Describe what happened in the clip.

How is the problem Francisco said that he could not solve different from the symbolic problem he posed and solved? Why might he be able to solve one but not the other?

What problem might you pose next?

How would you expect Francisco to react to the following problem?

If you had four pizzas, and you ate one eighth of a pizza, how much pizza would be left?

Analysis. In Part 1, Francisco said that he could not solve 4 − 1/8. He explained that he had previously solved only problems with *mixed numbers* (not Francisco's words but the numbers used in his example), gave the example $4\frac{3}{8} - 2\frac{1}{8}$, and quickly solved it. The novice interviewers were puzzled about why he could solve that problem but not the problem they had posed.

After Viewing Part 2 (2:06–3:51) of Video Clip #341 (Francisco, Grade 5, 3:51)

Describe Francisco's solution to the pizza problem.

How do you interpret the interviewer's reaction to his solving the pizza problem?

What might you do next to begin to build on Francisco's informal knowledge to link it to mathematics formalisms?

Analysis.   In Part 2, the interviewer posed the pizza problem and suggested that Francisco draw the four pizzas. Francisco partitioned one pizza into eighths and correctly answered the question posed. The interviewer told him that he had just solved the 4 – 1/8 problem. Francisco seemed surprised and pleased. Although the interviewer pointed out that the 4 pizzas could be the 4 in the symbolic problem and the 1/8 eaten could represent taking away 1/8 of a pizza, she, understandably, did not ask Francisco how he might represent his four pizzas with one partitioned in eighths symbolically other than as 4.

Note 1.   You can identify other video examples of the effect of context and the disconnection between children's informal and formal mathematics understandings by using the search term *in/out of context* within the *teaching/interviewing* search category.

STORY 2, Part III

Even deep understanding of a concept may be incomplete. Understanding can be extended.

In the video clip in Part III of this story, a student showed rich understanding of the meaning of division, seeing $a \div b$ as "How many bs are in a?" He used this understanding to solve a fraction-division problem with no remainder. He also correctly solved a problem with a remainder, but instead of writing the remainder as such, he wrote it as part of the quotient, not realizing that the remainder must be reconceptualized as a part of the divisor if it is written as part of the quotient. This example (Video Clip #321, Elliot, Grade 5, 1:29) illustrates that even deep understanding is likely to be incomplete; a teacher can build on the understanding a student has and extend it to even deeper understanding. This clip can be viewed in two parts.

Before Viewing Part 1 (0:00–0:40) of Video Clip #321
(Elliot, Grade 5, 1:29)

You are about to watch a fifth grader, Elliot, consider the following problem:

$$1 \div 1/3$$

How might a child solve this problem without using a standard algorithm?

After Viewing Part 1 (0:00–0:40) of Video Clip #321
(Elliot, Grade 5, 1:29)

Describe Elliot's thinking.

What did you learn about Elliot's understanding?

Analysis.   Elliot used his knowledge of the meaning of division to solve this problem. Elliot's answer is correct, and he showed understanding of the meaning of $a \div b$. He related his drawing to the symbols.

Before Viewing Part 2 (0:40–1:29) of Video Clip #321 (Elliot, Grade 5, 1:29)

> You are about to watch Elliot now consider the following problem.
>
> $$1\frac{1}{2} \div 1/3$$
>
> How do you expect Elliot to solve this problem?
>
> In what ways is this problem different from the first problem he solved: $1 \div 1/3$?

Discuss the ways this problem differs from the first problem Elliot solved. Consider possible sources of difficulty Elliot faced in solving this problem.

After Viewing Part 2 (0:40–1:29) of Video Clip #321 (Elliot, Grade 5, 1:29)

> Describe Elliot's thinking.
>
> What did you learn about Elliot's understanding?
>
> How would you respond if Elliot had written for his second answer 4 R 1/6?
>
> When working with rational-number multiplication or division, one must attend to the change of the unit. Explain how this issue is raised in this video clip.
>
> How would one reconceptualize the remaining 1/6 to answer $4\frac{1}{2}$? Why is this reconceptualization needed in this division problem?

Analysis.   Although Elliot's solution is not correct as written, he has recognized that there are four 1/2 s (of 1) in $1\frac{1}{2}$ with 1/6 (of 1) remaining. To incorporate this remainder as part of the quotient, one must consider what part 1/6 (of 1) is of another 1/3. Because 1/6 is 1/2 of 1/3, the quotient is $4\frac{1}{2}$.

Note.   For an expanded treatment of the mathematics of Elliot's problem, see Story 2: Appendix.

STORY 2: Appendix
Reconceptualizing the Remainder in Division
of Fractions as Part of the Quotient

When performing division *procedures*, one applies rules specific to division of whole numbers, fractions, or decimals. In considering a *context* in which division is applicable, how does the division relate to the context? Division contexts generally entail a total number, a number of groups, and the size of each group. A widely used distinction is between measurement (repeated subtraction or quotitive) division and partitive (or sharing) division: In a measurement context (e.g., *Twenty children are to be placed on teams of four children each. How many teams will be formed?*), the number of groups is unknown. In partitive division (e.g., *Twenty M&M's candies are to be shared equally by 4 children. How many M&M's candies will each child get?*), the size of each group is unknown. In the domain of whole numbers, each type of context is generally relevant for children.

In the fractions domain, however, measurement contexts accessible to children (e.g., *Rhoda has $3\frac{1}{2}$ cups of brown sugar. Her favorite cookie recipe takes 2/3 cup of brown sugar. How many recipes of these cookies can she make if she uses all the brown sugar she has?*) seem more natural than partitive contexts because a fractional number of groups is problematic in most such contexts. With young children, one does not generally speak of $3\frac{1}{2}$ teams or children.

Note that fraction values for the total number, the size of the group, or both are natural for children in partitive-division contexts in which the number of groups is a whole number (e.g., *If five children share equally $12\frac{1}{2}$ large cookies, how much cookie will each child get?* or *How much cookie will each child get if three children share four cookies equally?*). Such sharing scenarios can help children make sense of fractions.

The caution that partitive contexts in which the number of groups is a noninteger are seldom relevant for children does not preclude using fractions in, for example, a rate context. In the problem *John rode his bike $23\frac{3}{4}$ miles in $4\frac{1}{2}$ hours. What was his average rate?*, one could think of the $4\frac{1}{2}$ hours as the number of groups equally sharing the $23\frac{3}{4}$ miles to determine the rate, the number of miles per hour John rode. But a child-friendly partitive-division context in which the number of groups is a noninteger is difficult to create. A measurement problem can be reworded so that the number of groups is missing, but such problems generally seem contrived (e.g., *Rhoda had $3\frac{1}{2}$ cups of brown sugar and, using all the brown sugar she had, was able to make $5\frac{1}{4}$ recipes of her favorite cookies. How much brown sugar did she need for each recipe?*).

Reconceptualizing the remainder in division of fractions as part of the quotient is about meanings of division and meanings of fractions. Each of these topics is complicated so considering them together in a meaningful, versus strictly procedural, way leads to one of the more complex ideas in elementary school mathematics: division of fractions.

Purpose

A child coming to understand division of fractions from a conceptual point of view instead of learning an algorithm for fraction division understands some, but not all, aspects of division of fractions. In examining the work of this child, prospective and practicing teachers have opportunities to grapple with the complex idea of considering the remainder in division of fractions initially as part of the original whole and reconceptualizing it as a part of the divisor to include it in the quotient.

Activity

Students solve and discuss problems and watch video to prepare them to think about Elliot's solution for $1\frac{1}{2} \div 1/3$.

1. *If Pat wants to bake as many cookies as she can for the PTA bake sale and has 8 cups of flour on hand, how many recipes of her favorite chocolate chip cookies can she make if the recipe calls for 2 cups of flour?*

   How many groups of 2 are there in a group of 8?

The point of 1 is to present a measurement-division problem in which the size of the group is given and the answer is the number of groups. This whole number problem will set the stage for the following fraction measurement-division tasks:

2. *Pat discovers that she has only 1 cup of brown sugar, and her recipe calls for 1/3 cup of brown sugar. Now how many recipes can she make?*

   Students solve the problem.

   Imagine a child who correctly solves the problem but has yet to learn an algorithm for dividing fractions. How might the child solve the problem?

   Discuss possible solutions students suggest.

   Students examine and discuss Elliot's written work for $1 \div 1/3$.

   Watch and discuss Video Clip #321, 0:00–0:39.

   How many 1/3s are in 1?

3. If she had $1\frac{1}{3}$ cups brown sugar, how many recipes calling for 1/3 cup brown sugar could she make?

   How do you think Elliot would think about this problem?

4. *If she had $1\frac{1}{2}$ cups brown sugar, how many recipes calling for 1/3 cup brown sugar could she make?*

   Solve this problem.

   Solve this problem as you think Elliot might solve it.

   How is this problem different from $1\frac{1}{3} \div 1/3$?

   Discuss.

   Examine and discuss Elliot's work for $1\frac{1}{2} \div 1/3$.

   Watch and discuss Video Clip #321, 0:40–1:26.

5. *How would you describe Elliot's thinking about this problem? Is he correct? What understandings of division and of fractions does Elliot demonstrate? How might you respond to Elliot when he finished this problem?*

6. *How is the extra 1/6 cup of brown sugar treated differently in Elliot's answer and in the answer $4\frac{1}{2}$ for $1 \div 1/3$?*

STORY 3
Procedural and Conceptual Understanding

Although most educators agree that students need to develop both conceptual and procedural understanding of the mathematics they study, some question the importance of developing conceptual understanding before introducing procedures. By having students invent their own strategies, based on their understanding of numbers, teachers can ensure that conceptual knowledge is developed. Some teachers then use that understanding of number and operations to give meaning to standard procedures. Others avoid teaching standard procedures, encouraging children to refine their own strategies to become more and more efficient. Research by Pesek and Kirshner (2000) showed that teaching procedures before students had conceptual understanding of geometry topics interfered with their learning the content. In spite of devoting more than twice as much instructional time to learning the geometry content, those who were taught procedures before concepts learned less than those who first studied concepts. (We recognize that, when teaching procedures, teachers may link the procedures to concepts. However, because mathematics instruction in the United States generally focuses on teaching procedures without providing students with opportunities to connect these procedures to the underlying concepts, we consider the results of Pesek and Kirshner's study relevant.) Because this question of the order for teaching concepts and procedures seems of great importance, we designed a small study in which a teacher who normally begins with conceptual instruction before introducing procedures would, for one topic, reverse the order of her instruction.

In this story, we use video clips to show the effects, in that small study, of introducing procedures for converting between mixed numbers and improper fractions before helping students develop conceptual understanding of those processes. Students were interviewed approximately 2 weeks after the procedural lesson and again 2 weeks after the conceptual lesson. The teacher was interviewed as well. In addition, a paper-and-pencil assessment was administered to the whole class at four points: immediately after the procedural lesson, approximately 2 weeks later, immediately after the conceptual lesson, and, finally, approximately 2 weeks after that second lesson. The items and results of these assessments are shown in Table 1 (Philipp & Vincent, 2003). Notice that although the post procedural scores are about the same as the post conceptual scores, the delayed procedural scores are generally lower than the delayed conceptual scores, indicating that students may learn procedures to solve problems, but they tend to forget the procedures they have learned much more than they forget concepts they have learned.

TABLE 1.   Class Percentages of Correct Assessment Responses Immediately (Post) and 2 Weeks After (Delayed) the Procedural and Conceptual Lessons

Item	Problem	Post procedural ($n = 28$)	Delayed procedural ($n = 28$)	Post conceptual ($n = 29$)	Delayed conceptual ($n = 29$)
1	$8/3 =$	89	79	89	89
2	$10/6 =$	85	71	86	89
3	$6\frac{4}{5} =$	71	36	83	70
4	$3\frac{3}{8} =$	85	32	70	62
5	How many eighths are in five wholes?	67	71	89	93
6	Circle the larger number or put = if they are the same. $5/3$ $1\frac{2}{3}$	75	57	79	79

STORY 3, Outline

Part 0. Ask teachers to interview several students on a procedure that the students can perform and for which the teachers think the students understand the underlying mathematics.

Part I. The procedural lesson was based on a lesson from a state-adopted textbook. Students completed a paper-and-pencil assessment for converting between mixed numbers and improper fractions immediately after the lesson. (1 video clip)

Part II. Students interviewed 2 weeks after the procedural lesson were confused, either about how to perform the conversion or how to explain. (3 video clips)

Part III. The conceptual lesson was taught. Students completed a paper-and-pencil assessment for converting between mixed numbers and improper fractions immediately after the lesson. (1 video clip)

Part IV. Students interviewed 2 weeks after the conceptual lesson had greater understanding, but one student described the effect on her of having first learned the procedures instead of first "figuring it out" for herself. (2 video clips)

STORY 3, Part I

A teacher who usually teaches helps her students build concepts before introducing procedures, reversed her approach (at our request) and taught a procedural lesson for converting between improper fractions and mixed numbers.

The teacher of this lesson usually builds concepts, using a child-centered approach, before introducing procedures. In one instance, however (as part of an experiment), she taught a procedural lesson for converting between improper fractions and mixed numbers before she had introduced the topic in her usual way. This traditional lesson was based on a state-adopted-textbook lesson.

On a paper-and-pencil postassessment for converting between mixed numbers and improper fractions administered immediately after the procedural lesson, students' average scores per item ranged from 71% to 89%. On a question that required some knowledge of fractions, only 67% could give the number of eighths in five wholes (see Table 1).

STORY 3, Part I, Clip

Before Viewing Video Clip #518 (June's Class, Procedural Lesson, Grades 5–6, 5:58)

> How do you (or would you) teach students to convert between improper fractions and mixed numbers? What understanding of fractions should precede this instruction?
>
> The clip you are about to watch shows one approach to teaching this content.

Discuss the approaches suggested before viewing the video clip. Do not mention the procedural/conceptual distinction. Allow participants to raise the issue.

After Viewing Video Clip #518 (June's Class, Procedural Lesson, Grades 5–6, 5:58)

> Describe the lesson you saw in the video.
>
> What is your reaction to this lesson?
>
> After this lesson, how successful do you expect students to be in completing a paper-and-pencil assessment of converting between improper fractions and mixed numbers?

Analysis. In this clip, the teacher, following a lesson from a state-adopted textbook, minimally motivated converting between improper fractions and mixed numbers with an example of converting 9 quarts to gallons. She showed the procedure for converting the improper fraction to a mixed number and then showed, step by step, the procedure for converting a mixed number to an improper fraction. She posed the following question to conclude the part of the lesson shown in the clip: "When we're doing this, suppose you get zero as the remainder, when you divide a numerator by a denominator. What would that tell you?" One child may understand, but his explanation lacked clarity. Another student explained clearly. In describing this lesson, the teacher noted that the lesson had little, if anything, to do with fractions. It was merely about the steps one performs in completing the conversions, which her students performed willingly, in spite of the unusual approach for this teacher in this lesson, which she called *traditional.*

STORY 3, Part II

Retention was assessed, and some students were interviewed approximately 2 weeks after the procedural lesson.

Approximately 2 weeks after the procedural lesson, on a paper-and-pencil assessment for converting between mixed numbers and improper fractions, class-average scores ranged from 32% to 79% per item (see Table 1).

Some students were interviewed at this time. Although some had difficulty remembering the conversion procedures (e.g., see Video Clip #324, Everett, Grade 5, 1:29) , at least one child could complete the procedure, but she was unable to explain (Video Clip #362, Markie, Grade 5, 2:26). In one particularly telling interview, a child, Rachel, explained that she "cannot remember because she did not get to figure out [the procedure] for herself" (Video Clip #367, Rachel, Grade 5, 1:20).

STORY 3, Part II, Clips 1, 2, and 3

Video clips are provided for three of the students interviewed between the procedural and conceptual lessons on renaming fractions.

Before Viewing Video Clips #324 (Everett, Grade 5, 1:29), #362 (Markie, Grade 5, 2:26), and #367 (Rachel, Grade 5, 1:20)

> You are about to watch interviews of three of the students from the class on converting between improper fractions and mixed number. These interviews took place approximately 2 weeks after the lesson you viewed. They will be asked to rename fractions and explain the mathematics of their conversion procedures. How successful do you expect the students will be?

Discuss expectations for the students' success in renaming fractions and explaining their procedures.

After Viewing Video Clips #324 (Everett, Grade 5, 1:29), #362 (Markie, Grade 5, 2:26), and #367 (Rachel, Grade 5, 1:20)

> Describe what each child did in the video.
>
> Describe your reaction.
>
> Compare the experience of the traditional lesson for Markie and Rachel.
>
> Rachel's score on the paper-and-pencil assessment administered immediately following the traditional lesson was 85%. Her score on the delayed assessment was 16%. Comment.
>
> Do you have students like Markie? Do you have students like Rachel?

Analysis.   Everett converted $3\frac{1}{8}$ to 3/8. He used the whole number as the numerator of the improper fraction. He was unsure what happened to the 1 in 1/8.

Markie knew that 9/5 is an improper fraction and converted it correctly to a mixed number, which she read correctly, $1\frac{4}{5}$. When asked why she converted in that way, Markie said, "Because that's how I remember doing it when I was taught in . . . like when I was first taught to do it." When asked how she might explain why she did it that way to a younger sibling, Markie merely repeated the steps, "because 9 is bigger than 5."

Rachel was asked to convert $3\frac{3}{8}$ to an improper fraction. She said, "Okay," but then continued: "We did this before. But I don't exactly remember it as well, because I didn't figure it out for myself." When asked to explain that comment, Rachel said that when she figures out how the teacher got an answer, "It's easier. . . . And once I figure it out, . . . it stays there, because I was the one who brought it there. . . . It's just easier to do, when you figure it out yourself." Rachel recognized that the lesson on converting between mixed numbers and improper fractions was different from the usual mathematics lessons in this class: "And then this little time, it was different. And it was harder." She had a vague recollection that "8 had to be like divided by the 3 or something like that or . . . I don't remember," remembering the first step for converting in the other direction—an improper fraction to a mixed number.

STORY 3, Part III

The teacher who taught the procedural lesson for renaming fractions now taught a conceptual lesson on this topic, the lesson she would usually teach first.

Several weeks after teaching the procedural lesson, the teacher taught the same content, renaming fractions, in her usual child-centered way.

STORY 3, Part III Clip

In this clip (Video Clip #518, June's class, conceptual lesson, Grades 5–6, 7:38), the teacher used pattern blocks to help students understand the processes for converting between improper fractions and mixed numbers. This lesson was conducted about 5 weeks after the first lesson this teacher taught on this topic.

After this lesson, on the immediate paper-and-pencil postassessment for converting between mixed numbers and improper fractions, students' average scores per item ranged from 70% to 89%. When asked the number of eighths in five wholes, 89% of the students answered correctly (Philipp & Vincent, 2003).

Before Viewing Video Clip #518 (June's Class, Conceptual Lesson, Grades 5–6, 7:38)

> What approach different from the one in the clip you viewed might you take in teaching the concepts involved in renaming fractions?

Discuss approaches one might take to build concepts for converting between improper fractions and mixed numbers. The teacher of this lesson stated that when children can see the relationships between mixed numbers and improper fractions, they can devise their own methods for converting between the two.

After Viewing Video Clip #518 (June's Class, Conceptual Lesson, Grades 5–6, 7:38)

Describe the lesson shown in this clip.

How does it differ from the first lesson on renaming fractions?

What is the teacher's role in this lesson?

After this lesson, how successful do you expect students to be in completing a paper-and-pencil assessment of converting between improper fractions and mixed numbers?

Analysis.   In the lesson excerpts shown in this clip, the teacher used the yellow hexagon pattern block as 1 whole and asked the students to form wholes from the other shapes, using all the same shape to form each whole. A student noted that the trapezoid is 1/2 because two trapezoids form one whole.

The class developed a table of the shapes, number of that shape that make 1 whole, and the fraction name for one of that shape.

The teacher moved to improper fractions by having the students build, in succession, 2/3, 3/3, and 4/3. Some children showed 4/3 as 1 hexagon and 1 rhombus. Students were asked to visualize and describe 7/4 (they had no pattern block for 1/4).

Students were asked to form $3\frac{1}{3}$, to name the number of thirds in $3\frac{1}{3}$, and to explain how they determined the answer. The clip concluded with Rachel's stating the procedure, which she had devised, for converting a mixed number to an improper fraction.

STORY 3, Part IV

Students interviewed following the conceptual lesson were able to rename fractions and explain their procedures, but for at least one student, the initial procedural instruction interfered with her thinking.

In Part IV of this story, see the three students interviewed approximately 2 weeks after the traditional lesson interviewed again about 2 weeks after the conceptual lesson.

Approximately 2 weeks after the conceptual lesson, on a paper-and-pencil assessment for converting between mixed numbers and improper fractions, class-average scores ranged from 62% to 89% per item, but 93% correctly named the number of eighths in five wholes (see Table 1).

Before Viewing Video Clip #323 (Everett, 0:56, Grade 5), Video Clip #361 (Markie, 2:26, Grade 5), and Video Clip #366 (Rachel, 3:59, Grade 5)

> You are about to watch the same three fifth graders you saw in Part II when they were asked to rename a mixed number (or improper fraction) approximately 2 weeks after the second lesson you watched. How do you expect their responses to compare with those you saw in Part II approximately 2 weeks after the first lesson you saw on converting between mixed numbers and improper fractions?

After Viewing Video Clip #323 (Everett, 0:56, Grade 5), Video Clip #361 (Markie, 2:26, Grade 5), and Video Clip #366 (Rachel, 3:59, Grade 5)

> Describe each child's thinking.
>
> Describe the differences in Everett's and Markie's explanations.
>
> Rachel's score on the paper-and-pencil assessment after the second lesson was 100%; her score approximately 2 weeks later was 67%. What is your reaction to this information?
>
> Why do you think that Rachel said, after drawing the 3 wholes and the 3/8, that she would multiply 3 × 3 before correcting herself with the interviewer's prompting?

Comment on the ordering of procedural and conceptual instruction.

Interview your students on a procedure that they can perform and for which you think they understand the underlying mathematics (if not included in Part 0, the preparation for using this story).

Note that Rachel had confidence in her sense-making procedure. See Clips #148 (Freddie, Grade 3, 2:32–6:15) and #155 (Gretchen, Grade 1, 5:42) for children who believed that their incorrect algorithmic approaches were correct even though they had clearly explained their own correct strategies.

Analysis.   Everett converted $3\frac{1}{8}$ to 25/8; during the conversion, he explained, without being asked to do so, that he multiplied 3 × 8 "because there's three wholes, and each of them has eight. So there would be twenty-four eighths." He explained that he added the 1 because of the remaining 1/8.

Markie quickly converted $3\frac{3}{8}$, seeming to use the procedure she was taught initially: She wrote the × and + after the $3\frac{3}{8}$, just as the teacher had done in initially teaching the procedure during the first lesson. Markie did not explain without being asked to do so; in fact, she paused after being asked to explain until prompted by the interviewer: "Tell me again what the 8 stands for." Markie then seemed to recognize the reason for multiplying 8 × 3: "So you would multiply it by, umm, the whole number to get how many pieces there are in three wholes." She did not continue until she was told that she was correct and was prompted to go on: "What would you do then?" She explained that she added the numerator on "because that's the pieces that are like the extra in the whole."

Rachel began converting $3\frac{3}{8}$ by using the procedure as she remembered it: She multiplied 3 × 3 and added the 8 to answer 17/8. She spontaneously, without indicating that she thought that her first answer was incorrect, began a second approach. She drew a whole and partitioned it into eighths, saying that she would have three of those. She drew the other two wholes but did not partition them; she drew the 3/8. Rachel said, while drawing, "One . . . 1, 2, 3. And then there's eight in each. And then there was three more. One, 2, 3, out of the other wholes."

Next she seemed momentarily confused, still thinking that she would multiply 3 × 3, as she had initially: "And then you just kind of, umm . . . it has to be 3 times 3, umm, because there's three wholes. Umm . . . so it has to be 3 right here, 3 right here. Or 8 right here, 8 right here, and 8 right here."

After Rachel said that she would try it again and paused, the interviewer prompted by asking how many parts were in the whole Rachel had partitioned, in each whole, and in the part she drew. Rachel answered and said that she had 27 eighths.

The interviewer asked whether Rachel could multiply something and add something in the mixed number $3\frac{3}{8}$ to get 27/8, and Rachel recognized the correct process. She justified this corrected conversion procedure by explaining, "Umm, eight is one whole, and there's three . . . three wholes. So there has to be 8 times 3, which is 24. And then you would have to add the remainders." She seemed confident that the 27/8 was the correct answer.

The interviewer asked Rachel why she first applied the rule even though she did not "quite remember it the right way." Rachel responded, "Well, because I was taught that first." She said that she would have preferred to have the lesson relating to the number of parts in a whole instead of the rule-based lesson first, "because I would have remembered how to do it the right way, and the correct way." She affirmed that having the procedural lesson first interfered with her learning.

Note. A draft of the article referenced herein can be found at www.sci.sdsu .edu/CRMSE/IMAP/pubs.html.

STORY 4
Developing Fraction Understanding

One approach to introducing fractions is to draw upon equal-sharing contexts in which teachers can leverage children's informal equal-sharing skills to support their development of fraction understanding (Empson & Levi, in press). We draw from work based on this effective technique for this story. We begin, however, with examples of the fraction understanding we encountered while interviewing fifth-grade students whose classroom experiences with fractions were traditional. We learned that many such children have conceptions of fractions that enable them to complete some tasks but that are inadequate when the child moves to general fraction situations.

Note. This story is longer than 2 hours. One could shorten it by choosing just the first two clips in Part I, showing the first clip in Part II without discussion, and choosing just one of the two clips suggested to illustrate the equal-sharing lessons in Part II. The omitted clips could be assigned as homework with the questions posed in the relevant Problem Files to be answered by participants in conjunction with viewing the assigned clips.

STORY 4, Outline

Part 0 or Part III. Ask participants to interview several students to learn the students' conceptions of fractions. Three assessment protocols are included in the Resources of the Searchable product. Perhaps for K–4 students they would choose tasks from one of the Equal-Sharing Task sets and for older students choose several of the bolded items in the Fraction Assessment (including especially the fraction-comparison tasks). General suggestions for conducting such interviews precede the items in the Fraction Assessment. Story 6 includes general interview rationale and suggestions for interviewing children.

Part I. Three students who have some fraction understanding but whose understandings are inadequate for the execution of various fractions tasks are shown. The first of these is an articulate child, described by her teacher as an average student in mathematics, from a high-performing school. On the basis of this information and assessments we have conducted with numerous students (see Story 4: Appendix A), we believe that many students share her conceptions. The second clip illustrates a common confusion about fractions that results when fractions are defined in "out of" language. The confusions these two children hold are evident only when the children are asked to compare fractions or make sense of the relative quantities represented by fractions. The third and fourth clips show a boy whose fraction procedures are flawed, but his conversion procedures provide correct answers in some instances, perhaps leading to his use of the procedures in general. (4 video clips)

Part II. In a 2-week summer experience after they had completed second grade, four children met with a teacher (not their own) for 10 sessions to explore ideas of fractions in equal-sharing contexts designed to build on their informal understandings and support conventional definitions of fraction and understandings of relative fraction size. Food items provided for the breaks between the two morning sessions held each day were used to discuss equal sharing. Manipulatives were used. Children used drawings and explained their thinking about various sharing scenarios. The list of problems the students solved over the 2 weeks is provided in Story 4: Appendix B. No algorithms or rules for fraction operations were introduced. In this story, a video clip from the preinterview of one of the four children is selected to illustrate children's fraction conceptions before they engaged in the equal-sharing sessions. Video clips from two of the equal-sharing sessions show examples of activities in which the children engaged over the 2 weeks. Two video clips of the child whose preinterview thinking was included show her solutions to fractions items in an interview at the conclusion of the equal-sharing sessions and 2 years later. (5 video clips)

STORY 4, Part I

Students show partial understandings of fractions, especially of unit fractions, but they may overgeneralize these conceptions, leading to incorrect procedures and conceptions for fractions generally. Another issue is the misconceptions that arise when students interpret a common *out of* definition for fractions differently than teachers intend. Further, this definition is meaningless for fractions greater than 1.

In Part I, we show three students whose fraction understandings, although based on some correct ideas for unit fractions, lead them to erroneous thinking about fractions generally. The first of these students, Ally (Clip 1, Video Clip #302, Grade 5, 4:31, Part 1), is an articulate child from a high-performing school. In watching Ally's interview with us, Ally's teacher described Ally as about average in mathematics. On the basis of Ally's teacher's comment and assessments we have conducted with numerous students, we believe that her conceptions are shared by many students. However, teachers may be unaware of these confusions if children's work on fractions consists solely of performing fraction operations using standard algorithms. By simply asking students to compare fractions, one may discover confusions about fraction size that would lead to wondering about the benefits of correctly operating on numbers one misunderstands so profoundly. What meaning do the children hold for their answers? How are they to recognize whether their answers make sense if the quantities fractions represent are mysteries to the students?

The second clip (Video Clip #345, Jacky, Grade 5, 10:19) shows a child who holds a common confusion about fractions that results when fractions are defined in *out of* language, for example, speaking of 1/4 as "one out of four." The definition holds no confusion for a teacher. However, for the child shown in this clip, and many others we have encountered, this definition is fraught with difficulty. The student seems intuitively to realize that 2/7 of an area should be greater than 1/7 of the same area. However, Jacky alternates between this common-sense view and her understanding of the meaning of 1/7 as 1 *out of* 7, which she literally interprets as meaning that 1 piece is taken out of the 7. In this *out of* view, 2/7 is smaller than 1/7 because for 2/7, 2 of the 7 pieces (which may or may not be of equal sizes) are taken out and the areas remaining are compared in size. Thus the area or amount remaining when 2 of 7 parts are taken out of the whole is smaller than the area or amount remaining when 1 of 7 parts is removed from the whole. Again, this confusion becomes apparent when children compare fractions or make sense of the quantities represented by fractions. A further problem with the *out of* definition of fractions arises when one encounters fractions larger than 1. How can one take 7 pieces out of 6 pieces, the definition that would follow for 7/6? A definition that seems less likely to be misinterpreted by children is one in which the fraction is defined in terms of a unit fraction: If 6 equal-sized pieces form a whole, then one of those pieces is 1/6 of that whole; 5 of those pieces are 5/6 of that whole; 7 such pieces form 7/6 of that whole. (Note that the issue of the source of the 7 pieces is not problematic for unit fractions. If one conceptualizes subdividing a whole into 6 equal-sized pieces so that each piece is 1/6 of the whole, then one may also conceptualize 7 pieces each of size 1/6, and hence 7/6. However, when using "out of" language, one explicitly states that the 7 is taken out of the six, something that feels nonsensical to most people.)

The third and fourth clips (Video Clip #370, Sean, Grade 5, 1:35, and Video Clip #374, Sean, Grade 5, 1:32) show a boy whose fraction procedures are flawed, but his conversion procedures hold in some instances, perhaps leading to his use of the procedures in general. Sean's problems with fractions are not apparent in his fraction comparisons (he can be seen correctly comparing fractions in Video Clip #373).

Further evidence for the ubiquity of fraction misunderstanding in terms of number size can be found in the 12 clips in the Search Results for *content: fractions; strategy: number sense not evident.*

STORY 4, Part I, Clip 1

Before Viewing 0:50–3:01 of Video Clip #302 (Ally, Grade 5)

What understandings and misunderstandings did you find among your students in comparing fraction sizes?

The clip you are about to watch shows one student who exhibits at least three misunderstandings in comparing fractions, but each of her incorrect conceptions may be traced back to conceptions that had been correct when applied to more limited fraction contexts.

Before viewing this clip, discuss the fraction conceptions teachers saw in their interviews. If interviews were not conducted, discuss fraction conceptions one might expect to see in children whose understanding of fractions is limited. Note that this video clip was shot with two cameras, one focused on the interviewer and student and one focused on the student's workspace.

After Viewing 0:50–3:01 of Video Clip #302 (Ally, Grade 5)

Describe Ally's reasoning in comparing fractions.

Explain the conception Ally described in explaining each of these comparisons:

$$1/6 < 1/3 \qquad 1 > 4/3 \qquad 1/7 > 2/7 \qquad 3/6 < 1/2$$

What reasons that Ally gave to explain her fraction comparisons hold for some types of fractions (e.g., for unit fractions, larger denominators imply smaller fractions) but not for fractions generally? [Note other examples from the analysis below if participants do not provide the examples.]

What would you do next to help Ally revise each of her naïve conceptions so that her thinking would apply to fractions more generally?

Analysis.   At the beginning of this clip (0:20–0:24), Ally asked whether she should circle the bottom number and was told to circle the entire fraction. Whether a fraction is a representation of a single number for Ally is uncertain. In the clip viewed, the interviewer asked Ally, an articulate fifth grader, to compare fractions by circling the larger number in each pair. She initially compared the fractions as follows:

      1. $1/6 > 1/3$ **2.** $1 > 4/3$ **3.** $1/7 > 2/7$ **4.** $3/6 = 1/2$ **5.** $3/10 < 1/21/2$

While explaining her reasoning, Ally changed her answers for Items 1 and 4.

1. She said that she meant to say that $1/6 < 1/3$ because to change $1/3$ to $1/1$, a whole number, one needs to reduce the denominator of 3 by only 2, implying that to change the denominator of $1/6$ to $1/1$ would require reducing the denominator by 5. Thus, $1/3$ is closer to being a whole number than is $1/6$ and so is larger than $1/6$. Notice that for (a) unit fractions, (b) any two fractions between 0 and 1 with equal numerators (e.g., $3/5 < 3/4$), or (c) any two fractions between 0 and 1 with equal denominators (e.g., $2/5 < 3/5$), her reasoning is correct. In each of these instances, the fraction with the smaller difference between numerator and denominator is the larger fraction.

2. Ally implied in explaining why $1/6 < 1/3$ that whole numbers are larger than fractions, but in explaining why she thought that $1 > 4/3$, Ally stated this belief more clearly: "I thought 1 was bigger, because it's a whole number." Of course, students first encounter fractions as representing parts of a whole, so they represent quantities less than 1. (This notion that fractions are always less than 1 is also reflected in our natural language. For example, when a person says, "Only a fraction of the auditorium was occupied," we understand that most of the seats were empty.)

3. Although one might anticipate that Ally's reasoning in explaining why $1/6 < 1/3$ would lead to her correctly comparing $1/7$ and $2/7$, another common misconception leads her astray: "I chose one seventh, because I thought it was just the smallest number. And usually you go down to the smallest number to get to the biggest number [in fractions]." This notion is commonly heard expressed as "bigger makes smaller in fractions," another idea that is correct for the denominators in unit fractions or for common fractions with equal numerators; it does not, however, apply for fractions with equal denominators but is often misapplied in such contexts. (See Clip 2 in this section for another problem source for miscomparing fractions with equal denominators.)

4. Although Ally initially recognized the equality of $3/6$ and $1/2$, in explaining her reasoning, she chose $1/2$ as larger and reverted to her explanation for the first item. Because 1 and 2 differ by only 1, Ally may automatically choose $1/2$ as the larger in most comparisons.

5. The interviewer has recognized Ally's pattern in reasoning that $1/2$ is generally the larger of two common fractions, which she again explained in saying, correctly, that $3/10 < 1/2$. He asked Ally to compare $1/2$ and $4/6$ to illustrate this pattern. Ally, true to form, incorrectly chose $1/2$ as larger in this pair and reasoned as before.

STORY 4, Part I, Clip 2

Before Viewing Video Clip #345 (Jacky, Grade 5)

> What definitions of fractions do you hear from students? What are the affordances and constraints of various fraction definitions?
>
> The clip you are about to watch shows one student who exhibits confusion in comparing fractions with equal denominators. Unlike Ally (shown in Clip 1 in this section), Jacky is confused because of a definition that many children are taught. How might defining 2/7 as 2 out of 7, lead one to conclude that 1/7 > 2/7?

Before viewing this clip, discuss fraction definitions and their possible interpretations. Consider how a child might interpret 2/7 as "2 out of 7 parts."

After Viewing Part 1 (0:00–0:15 and 0:53–2:10) of Video Clip #345 (Jacky, Grade 5)

> Describe Jacky's comparison and her reasoning in comparing 1/7 and 2/7 when she concluded that 1/7 > 2/7.
>
> How is that reasoning consistent with the definition of 2/7 as "2 out of 7 parts"?

Analysis.   Jacky first circled 2/7 as being larger than 1/7. After being asked by the interviewer to use a rectangular representation for the two fractions, Jacky changed her answer and explained that 2/7 is less than 1/7 "because [for 2/7] you take away two pieces." When a second interviewer asked for more explanation, Jacky said, "The ones that are shaded in, you take them away because you probably already broke it and gave it to your friend or you might have ate it already."

After Viewing Part 2 (2:28–7:27) of Video Clip #345 (Jacky, Grade 5)

> Describe Jacky's reasoning in comparing 1/5 and 2/5 when she initially concluded that 2/5 > 1/5.
>
> How did her explanation change when she was reminded of her conclusion in comparing 1/7 and 2/7?
>
> How did Jacky's and the interviewer's naming of the fractions differ consistently? What conclusion about the way Jacky viewed fractions might one conclude from that difference?
>
> How did the introduction of the cookie context seem to affect Jacky's thinking?
>
> What do you think Jacky would have said the next day if asked to compare 1/5 and 2/5?

Analysis. Jacky circled 2/5 as the larger of 2/5 and 1/5 and explained her reasoning: "Because on the one fifth, you only get **one piece of a fifth.** And on this piece—on this one [2/5], you get **two pieces of a fifth.**" She confirmed this thinking with drawings. When the second interviewer reminded Jacky that she had answered the opposite way earlier, Jacky reverted to her previous thinking, saying both that $1/7 > 2/7$ and $1/5 > 2/5$.

The interviewers raised with Jacky the distinction between the shaded parts and the unshaded parts of the wholes and discussed which was being named. Jacky named the unshaded part in her representation for 1/5 as 4/5 and for 2/5 as 3/5. She first said that 4/5 was the larger. When questioned by the interviewer, she changed her answer but upon reflection, settled on 4/5 as larger than 3/5 "because **you get more pieces out of four fifths.**"

The first interviewer tried to move Jacky toward conventional thinking about the fractions by introducing the context of eating 1/5 of a cookie one day and 2/5 of a cookie the next. In that context, Jacky said that she would be eating more cookie when eating 2/5 than when eating 1/5 of a cookie.

Throughout the interview, Jacky's language in referring to fractions indicated that she was thinking of pieces not necessarily related to a whole. She consistently talked in terms of "How many pieces?" instead of in terms of "How much?" or "What part of the whole?" This situation is indicated in the language bolded above and in Jacky's responses to several questions from the interviewer. Notice that even after the interviewer restated Jacky's answer of "two" in the more fraction-oriented language of "two fifths," Jacky's immediately subsequent fraction answer was still stated as a whole number ("one") instead of as a fraction (one fifth) (3:30–3:35):

Interviewer:	And then, so how much is shaded on this bar?
Jacky:	Two.
Interviewer:	Two fifths? And then how much on this one?
Jacky:	One.
Interviewer:	One fifth.

After Viewing Part 3 (7:28–7:40 and 8:47–9:41) of Video Clip #345 (Jacky, Grade 5)

> How does the instructor explain the common error demonstrated when children say that $1/7 > 2/7$?
>
> How does she suggest that this error might be avoided?

Analysis. Jacky's interview took place during a course for prospective teachers in which the college students interviewed children regarding their mathematical thinking. The interviews were designed to investigate the children's thinking rather than to change it. Just as Jacky's interviewers encountered her confused thinking about which part of the whole is being named when one speaks of 1/7 as "1 out of 7," at least one other prospective teacher faced this challenge. The course instructors elaborated on the issue and suggested that a definition of 1/7 is as "one of seven equal pieces that make up one whole" would be less confusing to students.

STORY 4, Part I, Clip 3

Even though Sean correctly compared fractions (see Clip #373), he did not use his apparent understanding of relative number size to consider the relationship of his sum and the addends in his procedure for 1/2 + 1/3.

Before Viewing Video Clip #370 (Sean, Grade 5, 1:35)

> What errors might you expect in a student's solution for 1/2 + 1/3?

Before viewing this clip, discuss errors one might expect to see in the addition algorithm for this problem.

After Viewing Video Clip #370 (Sean, Grade 5, 1:35)

> Describe Sean's strategy for adding 1/2 + 1/3.
>
> How might you induce disequilibrium related to the fact that Sean converted each of the addends to the same fraction?
>
> How might you encourage Sean to consider the relationship of his sum to the addends, that is, to consider whether his answer makes sense?

Analysis. Sean recognized that the least common denominator (lcd) for the two fractions he was adding was 6 and mentally completed the procedure, without changing the numerators, to get a sum of 2/6. He did not notice that he had changed these unequal fractions to the same value: He changed each to 1/6. Further, his sum was equivalent to the smaller of the two addends. Even when asked twice by the interviewer whether he needed to do anything to the numerators, he said that he did not—except to add them. When asked to show the work for his addition, Sean showed his procedure for determining the lcd for 2 and 3. When the interviewer wrote the 1/6 + 1/6 below the original addends, the expression she had expected Sean to write, he confirmed that he had used that approach. Perhaps the interviewer had hoped that seeing the 1/6 below each of the differing addends would prompt Sean to realize that they should not both be equal to 1/6 or that neither equals 1/6. Earlier in the same interview from which this clip is taken, the interviewer had seen Sean correctly compare 1/6 and 1/8 as well as 3/6 and 1/2, so she may have been thinking that if Sean were thinking about fraction size, the equivalency of 1/6 and 1/2 and of 1/6 and 1/3 would be problematic for Sean. Sean's thinking was not affected by these interviewer moves, and she did not choose to be more direct in this assessment interview.

STORY 4, Part I, Clip 4

Even though Sean correctly compared fractions (see Clip #373), he did not consider the relationships between the mixed numbers and improper fractions when he converted from one to the other.

Before Viewing Video Clip #374 (Sean, Grade 5, 1:32)

In this clip, Sean is asked to convert $4\frac{1}{3}$ to an improper fraction. His procedure yields the improper fraction 5/3. What was his procedure?

Sean is next asked to convert 13/6 to a mixed number. His procedure for this conversion is more complex than his procedure for renaming a mixed number but is equally flawed.

Before viewing this clip, discuss the procedure Sean might have used to convert from a mixed number to an improper fraction and how he could have come to use such a procedure.

After Viewing Video Clip #374 (Sean, Grade 5, 1:32)

Describe Sean's strategy for converting $4\frac{1}{3}$ to an improper fraction.

Describe Sean's strategy for converting 13/6 to a mixed number.

Apply Sean's procedure to rename $8\frac{5}{6}$ as an improper fraction.

Is Sean's conversion procedure for improper fractions always reversible as it is in renaming 13/6?

How would you try to help Sean recognize that his procedures are incorrect?

Analysis. Sean first converted $4\frac{1}{3}$ to 5/3 by adding the whole number and the numerator and writing that sum as the numerator for his improper fraction, with the original denominator as the denominator of the improper fraction. He did not consider that 5/3 is too small to represent the quantity represented by $4\frac{1}{3}$. However, he may have no idea that the quantities represented by the improper fraction and the mixed number should be equal.

Sean's procedure for converting an improper fraction to a mixed number is more complex than his procedure for renaming mixed numbers. He first subtracted the denominator from the numerator (or counted up, as he explained). We interpret his explanation for adding 1 to the 7 (13 – 6) when he said, "It would be one whole left over, so then I took 1 more," as meaning that because 7 is more than 6, he added 1 more whole to 7 to get the 8. He then subtracted the 8 from the original numerator to get the numerator for the fraction in the mixed number. Notice that if one uses Sean's procedure, his mixed number $8\frac{5}{6}$ converts back to the improper fraction from which it came, 13/6. According to our interpretation of Sean's procedure for renaming improper fractions, however, his 5/3 would not convert back to the $4\frac{1}{3}$ from which he derived it.

STORY 4, Part II

An approach to introducing fractions in a way that supports children's informal conceptions is to use equal-sharing contexts to build on these conceptions. Most children have had opportunities to share equally during their daily lives.

In a 2-week set of sessions with children who had yet to be introduced to formalisms of fractions, four children worked with a teacher in solving and discussing equal-sharing tasks (see the contexts used in Story 4: Appendix B) to develop their fraction understandings.

The first section of Part II is a video clip from the preinterview of one of the four children, Felisha (Video Clip #338, Felisha, Grade 2, 1:22), in which she showed evidence of holding misconceptions about fractions. (Note that other clips from this preinterview can be viewed: #336 and #339. Each video clip has an accompanying Problem file with questions for discussion.)

In the second section of Part II, two clips excerpted from the equal-sharing sessions the four children experienced are shown. In the first of these clips (Video Clip #510, Fraction kids, Grade 2, 6:01), the four children explored the meaning and naming of fractions in the context of doughnuts. In the second clip (Video Clip #509, Fraction kids, Grade 2, 3:19), the four children explored the concept of improper fractions in the context of apples. (Note that other clips, with accompanying Problem files with questions for discussion, from these equal-sharing sessions can be viewed: #333, Felisha; #507, #508, #511, and #512, Fraction Kids.)

In the third section of Part II is a video clip from Felisha's postinterview, held at the completion of the equal-sharing sessions (Video Clip #334, Felisha, Grade 2, 2:09). Felisha used drawings and fraction understanding to determine the amount of cookie left if one eats 1/4 of each of 6 cookies. (Note that other clips, with accompanying Problem files with questions for discussion, from this immediate postinterview can be viewed: #327, #328, #329, #330, #331, and #335.)

Finally, in the fourth section of Part II, a clip is included from Felisha's delayed postinterview held 2 years after the fraction sessions (Video Clip #325, Felisha, Grade 4, 3:10). In this clip, Felisha determined that one third of one fourth is one twelfth and that 1/4 + 1/12 is 1/3. (Note that other clips, and accompanying Problem files, from this delayed postinterview can be viewed: #326, #327, #332, #337, and #340.)

STORY 4, Part II, Section 1

Felisha is one of the four children who participated in a 2-week experience in which an exemplary teacher conducted 2 sessions each day using equal-sharing contexts to help support children's informal conceptions of fractions derived from their own experiences with equal sharing. Each child was interviewed prior to the start of the experience. The children showed a range of understandings, but none had clear conceptions about fraction size and naming of fractions. In this clip, Felisha's naïve views of relative fraction size are shown.

Before Viewing Video Clip #338 (Felisha, End of Grade 2, 1:22)

> You are about to watch a child, Felisha, who at the end of second grade, before having instruction on fractions, is asked to compare fractions. How might a child with no formal instruction on fractions think about comparing the following: 2/4 and 1/2; 4/3 and 1; 3/6 and 5/8?

Discuss approaches to comparing fractions one might expect to see from children who have had no formal fractions instruction.

After Viewing Video Clip #338 (Felisha, End of Grade 2, 1:22)

> Describe what you saw in the video.
>
> Explain Felisha's strategy for comparing fractions.
>
> How might Felisha have come to reason about relative fraction size in this way?

Analysis. Felisha was asked to compare fractions. To compare 2/4 and 1/2, Felisha added the numerators and denominators and said that 2/4 is the larger of the two because 6 > 3. She used the same strategy to decide that 4/3 > 1 and that 5/8 > 3/6. She was asked to compare 5/4 and 1, but the viewer is left to decide what Felisha would say.

STORY 4, Part II, Section 2

Four children who had just completed Grade 2 participated in a 2-week experience in which an exemplary teacher conducted 2 sessions each day using equal-sharing contexts to help support children's informal conceptions of fractions derived from their own experiences with equal sharing. The teacher had the support of a research team in determining goals for the sessions, selecting tasks to achieve those goals, and debriefing about the effectiveness of the plan after each day's sessions. The list of equal-sharing contexts used each day is in Story 4: Appendix B. Between the two sessions each day, the children had a snack, often part of an equal-sharing discussion, and a walk outdoors. The teacher attended carefully to the children's ideas and built on those ideas.

STORY 4, Part II, Section 2, Clip 1

One topic that received extended discussion was whether the parts of a whole need to be the same size to be named with the same fraction. At one point, the teacher explained that for mathematicians, they do (in a part/whole model). Two examples of discussions from these sessions comprise this section of the story.

Before Viewing Video Clip #510 (Fraction Kids, End of Grade 2, 6:01)

> In this clip, four children discuss whether one piece of a doughnut cut into three pieces is 1/3 of the doughnut. What ideas might the children hold about this issue?

Discuss views of 1/3 of a doughnut one would expect to see from second graders who have had no formal fractions instruction.

After Viewing Video Clip #510 (Fraction Kids, End of Grade 2, 6:01)

> Describe what you saw in the video.
>
> Explain the conflicting views expressed.
>
> Was the issue resolved?
>
> What approach would you use to help children understand the importance of reasoning that in the parts-of-a-whole model all the thirds in the same sized whole should be the same size?
>
> Is the naming of these fractions a matter of convention or principle? [Whereas a principle is something that follows logically in a given situation, a convention is instead something upon which we mutually agree in the situation. The requirement that the thirds in a circle should be of equal size to be named *one third* is a convention we accept as part of the definition of *one third* in an area model of fractions.]
>
> In what fraction contexts can thirds of the same whole be unequal in size? [Conventionally, three elements in a set model need not be the same size to each be considered one third of the set. In a set model, we consider the number instead of the size of the objects to name the fractional parts of the whole set. In a set of three people, each, regardless of size, is conventionally considered one third of the set.]

Analysis.   The teacher began this session by cutting a doughnut in half. After she had cut one half in half again, three of the children thought that the halves of a half were thirds because each was one of three pieces comprising the whole. One child said that the three pieces must be equal in size to be called thirds. The children who said that the thirds could differ in size nevertheless called the one half "half."

The teacher tried to induce cognitive dissonance by having the children compare the sizes of the pieces they called thirds in the first doughnut to the three equal-sized pieces into which she cut another doughnut. She compared the sizes of the whole doughnuts, and the children agreed that the wholes were the same size. The three children insisted that each of the pieces could be called *one third* of the same sized whole even though the pieces themselves differed in size. One child maintained his stance that the pieces must be of equal size to be thirds of the same whole.

The teacher next cut a third doughnut into three pieces that differed in size even more than those in the first doughnut. Still three of the children said that each of those pieces is one third of the doughnut, even though they agreed that the distribution of those pieces would be unfair to the child who received the smallest piece. When the teacher asked if "thirds work that way, that they can be different sizes" (in the same whole), the fourth student said, "No. I don't think so."

STORY 4, Part II, Section 2, Clip 2

Children discussed fractions greater than 1.

Before Viewing Video Clip #509 (Fraction Kids, End of Grade 2, 3:19)

> In this clip, four children discussed the total number of eighths in apples cut in halves, fourths, and eighths. What issues would you expect to arise in this discussion? What important ideas about fractions could emerge from such a discussion?
>
> They considered the questions "Is 46/8 a real number?" and "How many whole apples are in 46/8?" How would you expect these children to answer these questions?

Discuss approaches to comparing fractions one might expect to see from children who have had no formal fractions instruction.

After Viewing Video Clip #509 (Fraction Kids, End of Grade 2, 3:19)

> Describe what you saw in the video.
>
> Explain Felisha's strategy for determining the number of whole apples in 46/8.
>
> With what important ideas about fractions have the children grappled during this session?

Analysis.   In this clip, children had in front of them apples cut into eighths, fourths, and halves, and they have one whole apple. In the context of leprechauns who could carry only eighths of an apple and who would trade gold for apples, the children determined the number of eighths of an apple in all the apples on the table. They counted up, by ones, from the 12 eighths they had, counting 2 for each of the fourths, 4 for each of the halves, and 8 for the whole apple on the table to arrive at 46/8. The teacher then asked whether 46/8 is a real number and asked the children to write it. Finally, she asked, "How many whole apples are in 46/8?" The children added 8s to arrive at 40/8 for five apples and 48/8 for six apples. They concluded that they would need 2 more eighths to have six apples.

STORY 4, Part II, Section 3

Felisha was interviewed on her fraction conceptions at the conclusion of the equal-sharing sessions. The children had not learned about algorithms for solving fraction problems.

Before Viewing Video Clip #334 (Felisha, End of Grade 2, 2:09)

> You are about to watch a child, Felisha, being interviewed at the end of second grade, after engaging in equal-sharing tasks with three other children for 2 weeks. How might she solve this problem:
>
> *Robert had six cookies. He ate one fourth of each cookie. How many cookies does Robert have left?*

Discuss approaches Felisha might take to solving this problem.

After Viewing Video Clip #334 (Felisha, End of Grade 2, 2:09)

> Describe what you saw in the video.
>
> Explain Felisha's strategy for solving the problem.
>
> What fraction understandings did Felisha show in her solution to this problem?

Analysis.   Felisha was asked to find the amount of cookie left if 1/4 of each of six cookies was eaten. She drew the six cookies, partitioned each into fourths, shaded 1/4 of each, and counted the remaining fourths to get 18/4. She counted off the one-fourths in groups of four and marked the number of cookies she had counted beside each fourth that yielded a whole cookie (i.e., after every fourth of the 1/4s). She had 4 sets of four 1/4s and two 1/4s left, so she answered $4\frac{1}{2}$.

STORY 4, Part II, Section 4

Felisha was interviewed on her fraction conceptions 2 years after engaging in the equal-sharing sessions with three other children. We have no information about her fraction instruction in school during her third and fourth grades.

Before Viewing Video Clip #325 (Felisha, End of Grade 4, 3:10)

> You are about to watch Felisha, now at the end of fourth grade, think about the following problem. Please solve it.
>
> *You and three friends are having a math party and you want to evenly share an award-winning cookie. You cut the cookie into four equal pieces. However, before you eat it, one of your friends gets a call and leaves without taking any cookie. You and your two friends decide that you want to eat all the cookie, but you each want the same amount. How might you cut the cookie, given that it has already been cut into four equal pieces?*
>
> *How much would you each get?*

Discuss solutions to this problem. Did any of the teachers give an answer using fraction language? If so, how did they reason about the problem?

After Viewing Video Clip #325 (Felisha, End of Grade 4, 3:10)

> Describe what you saw in the video.
>
> Explain Felisha's reasoning.
>
> What do you think about Felisha's reasoning?

Analysis. Felisha showed how each of four children would get 1/4 of a cookie but then was asked to find the amount each of three children would get if the fourth child left without eating any of the cookie after the cookie had been cut. She partitioned the fourth that was now to be shared among three children into thirds and explained that each child would now get 1/4 plus 1/12, which she realized is 1/3 of the cookie.

She explained that she knew that the 1/3 of 1/4 is 1/12 because partitioning each of the fourths into thirds would give 4 × 3 or 12 pieces. Did she know that the amount each child would get is 1/3 solely because three children were sharing the cookie equally? She seemed to be thinking of putting the 1/12 with each of the three 1/4s to see that each (1/4 + 1/12) makes 1/3 of the cookie. Although 2 years have passed since Felisha experienced the equal-sharing sessions with the other three children and she may have had other instruction on fractions during that time, she still used drawings constructively and seemed to think clearly about fractions size and relationships of parts to the whole in her reasoning about this problem and others we posed to her.

STORY 4, Appendix 1:
Grade 5 Data (*n* = 28)
High-Performing School

1) For each of the following number pairs, circle the larger number or write = if the numbers are equal.

a) 1/6 1/8	1/6	1/8	Equal	No Answer	% correct
	20	7	0	1	71

b) 1/7 2/7	1/7	2/7	Equal	No Answer	% correct
	5	21	1	1	75

c) 1/3 1/2	1/3	1/2	Equal	No Answer	% correct
	7	20	0	1	71

d) 1 4/4	1	4/4	Equal	No Answer	% correct
	5	1	21	1	75

e) 4/8 1/2	4/8	1/2	Equal	No Answer	% correct
	2	7	18	1	64

f) 4/3 1	4/3	1	Equal	No Answer	% correct
	9	16	2	1	32

g) 4/6 1/2	4/6	1/2	Equal	No Answer	% correct
	13	13	1	1	46

h) .52 .7	.52	.7	Equal	No Answer	% correct
	17	9	0	2	32

i) .3 .30	.3	.30	Equal	No Answer	% correct
	3	10	13	2	46

j) .8 .91	.8	.91	Equal	No Answer	% correct
	6	20	0	2	71

k) 1/7 .7	1/7	.7	Equal	No Answer	% correct
	5	11	10	2	39

2) Subtract 5 – 1/4 =	$4\frac{3}{4}$	Other (e.g., 1/1, 4/4, 4, 3/4, $3\frac{3}{4}$)		No Answer	% correct
	6	9		13	21

3) If you get 1/4 of 8 jelly beans, how many do you get?	2	half	4	Other (e.g., 6, 1, 1/4, 7, 32, $7\frac{3}{4}$)	No Answer	% correct
	11	4	3	7	3	39

4a) Draw a picture to show what 1/4 means.	4 nearly equal parts; one shaded (set or area model)		Unequal parts	Other (e.g., 4 parts with no shading; all shaded)	No Answer	% correct
	20		3	4	1	71

4b) Explain why your picture shows 1/4?	1 of 4 equal parts	1 of 4 parts	1 out of 4	Other	No Answer	% correct
	1	12	7	4	4	4

5) Add 0.52 + 0.7 =	1.22	0.59	5.9		No Answer	% correct
	15	11	1		1	54

6) Circle the best <u>estimate</u> for the sum 19/20 + 12/13.	1	2	31	33	none of these	No Answer	% correct
	2	5	2	7	10	2	18

7) Shade 60% of 10 × 10 grid.	Shade 6 columns	Shade 6 rows	% correct
	26	2	100

8) Shade 40% of 5 × 10 grid.	Shade 20	Shade 40	Other	No Answer	% correct
	12	13	2	1	43

9) If you had 5 pizzas and you ate 1/4 of one pizza, how much pizza would be left?	$4\frac{3}{4}$	3/4	$5\frac{3}{4}$	Other (e.g., $4\frac{1}{4}$, 4)	No Answer	% correct
	10	5	3	9	1	36

10) How much is one fourth of $60?	$15	$20	Other	No Answer	% correct
	17	2	5	4	61

11) If 4 children share 7 candy bars fairly, how much candy bar does each child get?	$1\frac{3}{4}$	1 r 3	$1\frac{1}{2}$	Other	No Answer	% correct
	3	3	4	16	2	11

12) One school has 120 fifth graders. If 25% of these fifth graders eat a hot lunch, how many students eat a hot lunch?	30	25	95	Other	No Answer	% correct
	11	2	3	5	7	39

13) Is the shaded part in the picture [square partitioned into 4ths, 1 part shaded] 1/4 of the square? If the shaded part is <u>not</u> 1/4, what fraction of the square is shaded?	Yes	No	No Answer	% correct
	27	1	0	96

14a) Is the shaded part in the picture [circle partitioned into halves, with half of one half shaded] 1/4 of the circle?	Yes	No	No Answer	% correct

	Yes	No	No Answer	% correct
	12	15	1	43

14b) If the shaded part is <u>not</u> 1/4, what fraction of the circle is shaded?	1/3	Other
	14ᵃ	3

Note. Four students answered the second question even though they had said that the shaded part is 1/4. The student who said it is not 1/4 said that 1 is shaded.

[a]Includes the response of the student who did not answer the first part of the question.

15a) Is the shaded part in the picture below 1/4 of the rectangle?	Yes	No	No Answer	% correct
	15	12	1	43

15b) If the shaded part is <u>not</u> 1/4, what fraction of the rectangle is shaded?	1/6	1/3	Other[a]	% correct
	6	3	6	21

Note. Some students who answered Yes to the first question still gave an answer to the second.

[a]One other response was that the pieces are unequal so the picture does not show any fraction.

16) Mark an X to show where 3/4 would be on this number line:	At $\approx 3/4$	At 3	At $\approx 3\frac{3}{4}$	Other	No Answer	% correct
	3	4	13	5	3	11

17) Mark an × to show where 1/4 would be on this number line:	At $\approx 1/4$	At 1	At $\approx 1\frac{1}{4}$	Other	No Answer	% correct
	4	5	4	12	3	14

STORY 4: Appendix 2
Fraction Problems by Day and Session

Summer 2000
Beginning–Grade 3 Students

Day 1		
Session 1	1.1	4 children share 12 stickers
	1.2	2 people share 7 cookies
	1.3	9 bagel pizzas are shared by 4 children
Session 2	2.1	8 children share 9 mini chocolate pies
	2.2	4 children share 10 chocolate bars (omitted)
	2.3	4 brownies are shared among 3 children
	2.4	6 divers share 20 bars of gold recovered from the Titanic wreckage
Day 2		
Session 3	3.1	3 children share 2 doughnuts
	3.2	6 people share 8 pancakes
	3.3	3 apples are shared by 4 children
Session 4	4.1	3 little pigs share 11 ears of corn
	4.2	2 children share half of a pie
	4.3	13 licorice sticks are shared among 8 children (omitted)
Day 3		
Session 5	5.1a	4 children share 5 doughnuts (doughnuts the same)
	5.1b	4 children share 5 doughnuts (doughnuts all different)
	5.2	4 people share 1 doughnut
	5.3	2 people share 1 doughnut
	5.4	3 people share 1 doughnut
	5.3	3 people share 2 doughnuts
Session 6	6.1	Make a whole in as many ways as you can.
		(Using fraction circles; not on paper)
Day 4		
Session 7	7.1	Make whole circles from three colors or fewer. Record your work. (Students used fraction circles: wholes, halves, thirds, fourths, sixths, eighths, twelfths)
Session 8	8.1	How many apples (on a tray with 3 halves, 7 fourths, and 12 eighths?
	8.2	How many eighths do we have for the leprechauns?

Day 5		
Session 9	9.1	8 children share 15 candy bars
	9.2	8 children share 15 candy bars (want large pieces)
	9.3	8 children share 15 candy bars (all different) (Used in Session 10)
Session 10	10.1	20 children each get three eighths of a pizza (Used in Session 11)
	10.2	5 children share 1 pizza at one table 7 children share 1 pizza at another table (Postponed to Session 12)
	10.3	3 children share 4 donuts; 6 children share? donuts (omitted)
	10.4	3 children share 4 brownies at one table 5 children share 8 brownies at another table (omitted)
Day 6		
Session 11	11.1	22 children each get two eighths of a pizza
Session 12	12.1	5 children share 1 pizza at one table 7 children share 1 pizza at another table
Day 7		

Session 13		Warm-Up (10–10:15)
		   Write one half; draw one half
		   Write two thirds; draw two thirds
		   Write five fourths; draw five fourths
		Palm Pilot (10:15–10:45)
		   Play game (10 minutes)
		   Group discussion of each item (20 minutes)
		     1. Write what fraction you think is shown and why you think that is the fraction.
		     2. Are there any other answers that would be correct? (equivalence)

Session 14		Pizza Problem (11–11:30)
		   18 people share 3 large pizzas
		    Issues
		     1. Naming (according to the size of the piece)
		     2. Equivalence (if someone's answer includes 1/3 of 1/8, ask how many pieces that size would fit in the whole pizza)
		     3. Improper fractions (How many 6ths in 3 pizzas?)

STORY 5
Mathematical Proficiency

People's beliefs about mathematics play a significant role in the approach they take to learning and teaching mathematics (Philipp, 2007). Students who believe that learning mathematics involves being shown how to apply well-specified procedures will hold different classroom expectations from students who believe that mathematics involves grappling with problems for which they are not given clear solution paths. Furthermore, teachers' approaches to teaching are also affected by their beliefs about mathematics. A teacher who views mathematics as fundamentally comprised of facts and procedures is likely to approach teaching as helping students memorize, remember, and apply facts and procedures, whereas a teacher who views mathematics as fundamentally comprised of ways of reasoning and problem solving is likely to approach teaching as providing students with many opportunities to grapple with complex, novel situations.

In 2001, the National Research Council (NRC), in defining mathematical proficiency as comprised of five interrelated strands taken together, presented a broader, more encompassing view of mathematics than that generally provided, The five strands are conceptual understanding, procedural fluency, strategic competence, adaptive reasoning, and productive disposition (Figure 1). This story is devoted to highlighting what these strands and the interrelationships among them might look like among children.

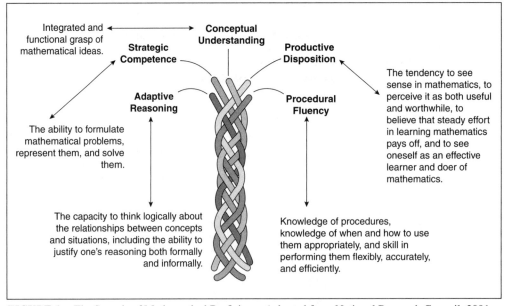

FIGURE 1.   The Strands of Mathematical Proficiency (adapted from National Research Council, 2001, p. 117).

STORY 5, Outline

Part I. Conceptual Understanding and Adaptive Reasoning: The Core of Sense-Making

Part II. Procedural Fluency: Is It More Than Knowing Procedures?

Part III. Productive Disposition: Making the Invisible Strand Visible

Part IV. Strategic Competence: What to Do When You Don't Know What to Do

STORY 5, Part I

Conceptual understanding and adaptive reasoning: The core of sense-making.

Conceptual understanding is defined as an "integrated and functional grasp of mathematical ideas" (NRC, 2001, p. 118), and the first part of the definition of adaptive reasoning is, "the capacity to think logically about the relationship among concepts and situations" (NRC, 2001, p. 129). Clearly, these two are closely related, because one could not hold an integrated grasp of ideas without thinking logically about the conceptual relationships. The second part of the definition of adaptive reasoning, "knowledge of how to justify the conclusions" (NRC, 2001, p. 129) by reasoning both formally and informally, is an important addition to mathematical proficiency, because it highlights that a learner must not only understand but must also be able to explain his or her reasoning. The two video clips in Part I (Video Clip #104 and Video Clip #158) highlight conceptual understanding, but only one (Video Clip #158) provides clear evidence that the child can justify his reasoning.

Before Viewing 0:00–1:10 of Video Clip #158 (Javier, Grade 5, 1:54)

You are about to watch a fifth grader, Javier, solve the following problem without applying an algorithm:

How many eggs are in six dozen?

How would you solve this problem without using an algorithm? How might a child solve it without applying an algorithm?

After Viewing 0:00–1:10 of Video Clip #158 (Javier, Grade 5, 1:54)

Describe Javier's reasoning.

Did Javier explain his reasoning?

Did anything surprise you about his reasoning?

Analysis.   Most people have not memorized multiplication facts for 12, but by thinking of 12 as 10 + 2, one can distribute the 6 and recognize that 6 × 12 = 60 + 12. This is the strategy we expect to see most often from adults who are not using an algorithm. Below is one way to symbolize Javier's reasoning, including the properties he invoked. (Note that we are not suggesting that Javier knew the names of the properties or that he would have represented his thinking in this way. We do suggest that Javier's reasoning might be represented more formally in this way. In other words, this is our representation of Javier's reasoning.)

$$
\begin{aligned}
&6 \times 12 \\
&= (5 \times 12) + (1 \times 12) && \text{Distributive property of} \times \text{over} + \\
&= [(1/2 \times 10) \times 12] + 12 && \text{Substitution property} \\
&= [1/2 \times (10 \times 12)] + 12 && \text{Associate property of} \times \\
&= [1/2 \times 120] + 12 \\
&= 60 + 12 \\
&= 72
\end{aligned}
$$

Few people would think to solve this task the way Javier did, which was as (5 + 1) × 12, or 5 groups of 12 and 1 group of 12. Furthermore, Javier's means for determining 5 × 12 (as 1/2 of [10 × 12]), though highly unusual, reflects rich number sense. Notice, too, that Javier clearly explained his reasoning, and in the process, he provided a type of justification. ("Five times a number might be conceptualized of as 1/2 of 10 times the number" is, simultaneously, an explanation for Javier's reasoning and a justification for why such an approach might be applied generally.)

The next video clip is of a younger child, Andrew, who solved a task using an unorthodox approach.

After Viewing 0:00–1:24 of Video Clip #04 (Andrew, Grade 2)

Describe Andrew's reasoning.

Did Andrew explain his reasoning?

When asked how he knew that he could rewrite 120 + 96 as 190 + 26, Andrew shrugged. How do you interpret his shrug? Do you think he understood the approach he used, or might this be a procedure he learned without understanding?

Analysis.   Andrew solved 120 + 96 by reconceptualizing the problem as 190 + 26. He was able to explain his solution in a manner that might be represented symbolically as shown below. (Note that, as in the case of Javier, we do not claim that Andrew would have represented the problem this way. We claim only that Andrew's reasoning might be represented formally by this symbolic representation.)

$$190 + 26$$
$$= 190 + (10 + 16) \qquad \text{Decomposition (based on place-value understanding)}$$
$$= (190 + 10) + 16 \qquad \text{Associative property of addition}$$
$$= 200 + 16$$
$$= 200 + (10 + 6) \qquad \text{Decomposition (based on place-value understanding)}$$
$$= (200 + 10) + 6 \qquad \text{Associative property of addition}$$
$$= 210 + 6$$
$$= 216$$

Andrew's place-value understanding guided him in knowing how to decompose and recompose the addends so as to simplify the calculations while holding the sum invariant, a solution that we believe demonstrates conceptual understanding. We have found that some teachers interpret Andrew's shrug as an indication that he is applying a procedure he has learned without understanding. (Because of other information we have about Andrew, we disagree with this interpretation. Andrew had not been shown how to decompose numbers in this way: he devised this solution on his own. But this fact may be irrelevant to the discussion.) This video clip provides a context for discussing the difference between students who provide clear justifications for their reasoning, and students who do not. The video clip also provides opportunities to discuss the distinction between providing an *explanation*, whereby one shares *what* one was thinking, and a *justification*, whereby one shares *why* one's thinking makes mathematical sense. Javier provided a justification for his reasoning, whereas Andrew did not.

(Note that a particularly illustrative example of adaptive reasoning is Felisha's reasoning in solving a fraction task, in Video Clip #325 [Felisha, Grade 4]. This video clip was included in Stories 1 and 4 and will be mentioned again later in this story.)

STORY 5, Part II

Procedural fluency: Is it more than knowing procedures?

Procedural fluency is defined as "knowledge of procedures, knowledge of when and how to use them appropriately, and skill in performing them flexibly, accurately, and efficiently" (NRC, 2001, p. 121). For many people, mathematics is comprised primarily, perhaps solely, of learning to apply procedures. Although thinking of mathematics *only* as procedures is problematic, procedural fluency should not be underestimated as an important component of mathematical proficiency.

Before Viewing Video Clip #195 (Rachel, Grade 5, 1:42)

You are about to watch a fifth grader, Rachel, use a nonstandard algorithm to multiply 45 × 36. Use an algorithm you know to multiply these numbers, and then try to devise second way to multiply these numbers.

Could your second way be used for any whole-number multidigit multiplication?

Analysis.   The difference between an algorithm and a strategy is that an algorithm is a general process for calculating with numbers, and it may be applied with any numbers. Algorithms are powerful because they are general and because they may be applied without understanding the underlying concepts. Society benefits because people have procedures for adding and subtracting with which they may calculate, for example, when balancing a checkbook, even if people cannot explain the mathematics underlying the algorithm. But in teaching, we want students to recognize not only how to perform procedures but also why they can be used, that is to understand the mathematics of the procedures.

After Viewing Video Clip #195 (Rachel, Grade 5, 1:42)

> Explain Rachel's procedure. Explain the mathematics of her procedure. Why is it correct?
>
> Compare the procedure Rachel used with the standard multidigit-multiplication procedure taught in the United States.

Analysis.   Rachel's multidigit-multiplication algorithm is more conceptually transparent than the standard algorithm because she makes explicit the role of place value throughout the procedure. However, even so, one might learn the algorithm Rachel used in a less meaningful way than Rachel, because, for example, instead of thinking "forty times thirty is one thousand, two hundred," one might think, "I multiply the 3 and the 4 and then I add 2 zeros because that's how I learned this." (Note that the algorithm Rachel applied to multiply whole numbers is structurally equivalent to the algebraic approach used in multiplying binomials, such as $(x + 3)(2x + 5)$.)

We do not suggest that our standard algorithm should be replaced by Rachel's algorithm. Instead, we use this clip to highlight that, for Rachel, her knowledge about how to use the procedure is integrated with her understanding of why it is correct, and we think that this is a higher level of mathematical proficiency than if she knew only how to use the algorithm without understanding the mathematics underlying it.

The next clip shows another child who efficiently applies an algorithm.

After Viewing Video Clip #156 (Hally, Grade 3, 2:27)

> Describe what Hally did and how she was thinking.
>
> Describe Hally's mathematical proficiency.

Analysis.   Hally clearly had memorized the procedure for subtracting multidigit numbers, and she applied the procedure efficiently. One could think about Hally's understanding in (at least) three ways. First, one might claim that she had procedural fluency because she knew which procedure to apply and she applied it efficiently and correctly. Second, one might claim that she did *not* have procedural fluency because one aspect of procedural fluency is knowing what to use and knowing when it is not necessary, and applying this procedure to subtract 1 from 1000 is akin to "using a nuclear bomb to kill a fly" (Guershon Harel, personal communication, September 19, 2010). A third stance is that Hally demonstrated procedural fluency but not mathematical proficiency. This third stance indicates that procedural fluency is more about knowing when and how to apply a procedure, whereas mathematical proficiency more generally involves a sense-making, integrated approach of concepts, procedures, problem solving, reasoning, and dispositions. When a student applies a procedure in a situation in which a significantly more efficient conceptual approach is available, this *nonexample* of conceptual understanding in the context of the procedure provides evidence that, at least with respect to this task, some component of mathematical proficiency is lacking.

However one classifies the understanding shown by Hally in this video clip, we suggest that mathematical proficiency should entail approaching mathematics as a sense-making endeavor, and although appropriately selecting a procedure and correctly applying it is a component of mathematical proficiency, learning to think more strategically and efficiently about mathematics tasks is an important component of mathematical proficiency. Hally provides an example of a student who used a procedure that was correctly applied, but superfluous. Similarly, students who estimate 8/9 + 11/12 by finding common denominators and adding the fractions, or who add 95 + 5 + 83 by writing the numbers vertically and using the standard algorithm, or who multiply 47 × 68 × 0 by first multiplying the 47 and 68 also provide nonexamples of conceptual understanding in the context of procedures and do not demonstrate rich mathematical proficiency.

STORY 5, Part III

Productive disposition: Making the invisible strand visible.

Productive disposition is defined as the tendency to see sense in mathematics, to perceive it as both worthwhile and useful, to believe that steady effort in learning mathematics pays off, and to see oneself as an effective learner and doer of mathematics. When people hear about productive disposition, they almost always agree that this strand is important. And yet, when asked whether they think that this strand was addressed in their mathematics education, most people respond that the strand seemed to be missing.

We think that the reasons productive disposition is so often missing from instruction are deeply entrenched in the culture of mathematics teaching and learning in the United States, and hence, we do not think that this situation can be quickly rectified. Yet, we also know of no way to approach this situation other than to bring this important strand to the attention of teachers so that they might recognize its importance in mathematics teaching and learning.

Earlier we viewed a video clip of Hally (Video Clip #156) solving 1000 − 1 using an algorithm. When asked about the meaning of the symbols, Hally did not connect the symbols to their place-value representations. By not connecting the procedure to the concept, Hally provided no evidence, for that task, that she saw the sense in mathematics, a component of productive disposition. The next video clip, of Johanna, shows a child who makes connections between and among all the strands of mathematical proficiency.

Before Viewing Video Clip #167 (Johanna, Grade 3, 4:31)

You are about to watch a third grader, Johanna, solve 1000 − 4 using an algorithm. She then answered questions about the algorithm. Consider the evidence that Johanna showed a productive disposition if *productive disposition* is defined as comprised of the following tendencies:

1) to see sense in mathematics;

2) to view mathematics as worthwhile and useful;

3) to believe that steady effort in learning mathematics pays off; and

4) to see oneself as an effective learner and doer of mathematics.

After Viewing Video Clip #167 (Johanna, Grade 3, 4:31)

Describe Johanna's reasoning.

What did you take as evidence for Johanna's productive disposition?

When describing her solution, Johanna said, "It's part of learning in school and also part of thinking" (pointing to her head when she said "thinking"). What distinction do you think Johanna was drawing between *school* and *thinking?*

Analysis. Johanna knew how to apply the standard multidigit-subtraction algorithm, and she was aware of the symbols' meanings. She provided evidence that her knowledge of the procedure was connected to her conceptual understanding. However, when the interviewer sought to determine the depth of Johanna's understanding by asking follow-up questions, Johanna's understanding was shaky. When asked what the new number was, Johanna responded, "I don't know what the new number is," and then, after thinking a little longer, she realized that it was 9, 9, 10. When asked whether the regrouping changed the value of the minuend (1000 became 9 9 10), Johanna responded that she was unsure. Johanna explained that the 9 9 10 digits represented hundreds, tens, and ones (respectively). She said, "I don't quite get this," and when the interviewer asked, "How many hundreds do you have," Johanna answered, "Nine," thought for a few seconds, and then, confidently stated, "Oh, I get it." She explained that she had 990, with 10 left. This video clip provides evidence that Johanna was trying to make sense of mathematics, and she clearly believed that steady effort in learning mathematics pays off. She also seemed to see herself as an effective learner and doer of mathematics, which gave her the confidence to continue grappling with a task that she did not immediately understand. Perhaps of all the noteworthy aspects of Johanna's reasoning, it is her willingness to continue thinking about something about which she was unsure that sets her apart from most people who do not possess strong productive dispositions toward mathematics. Johanna knew when she did not understand, and rather than discourage her from engaging, Johanna's knowledge of what she did not understand motivated her to continue grappling. Furthermore, her conceptual understanding, her procedural fluency, her adaptive reasoning, and her strategic competence are interconnected and together supported her while she pursued her sense-making stance toward mathematics.

Many video clips capture students who seem to possess productive dispositions, and many video clips capture students who do not seem to possess productive dispositions. Often, the child's stance is evident in his or her demeanor as much as in the child's thinking. Consider two boys, Eduardo, a fifth grader solving 4 shared among 3, and Gilberto, a third grader, solving a story problem requiring him to add 265 + 537.

Before Viewing Video Clip #316 (Eduardo, Grade 5, 3:02) and Video Clip #151 (Gilberto, Grade 3, 0:36)

You are about to view two video clips featuring Eduardo, a fifth grader, and Gilberto, a third grader. Both clips involve the students being asked to think about a task, but the similarities between the clips end there. Whereas Eduardo struggled to determine how 4 cookies might be shared evenly among three children, Gilberto drew upon his number sense to easily add 265 + 537. Eduardo was interviewed by a prospective teacher who had little interviewing experience whereas Gilberto was interviewed by an expert, but the differences in the children's approaches seem to have little to do with the interviewer.

While you watch each interview, make notes about each child's productive disposition. Attend to each child's reasoning and demeanor, including verbal and nonverbal cues.

Analysis. Gilberto confidently and competently solved the problem, drawing upon rich number-sense understanding, and he clearly explained his reasoning. His demeanor was positive when he leaned forward and smiled while talking. One has the sense that for Gilberto, mathematics makes sense, and he enjoys, even welcomes, challenges. Eduardo leaves a different impression. He seemed to understand what he was being asked and he used marks to represent the three children and the four cookies. He also understood that each child got one cookie and that the three children shared the fourth cookie; he partitioned the last cookie into six equal-sized pieces. Watching Eduardo, one has the sense that he has all the understanding required to solve this problem. Like Johanna, Eduardo was confused about something, but unlike Johanna, he did not seem to have the confidence that he could work through this confusion. Furthermore, his body language and his demeanor leave one with an impression of a child whose engagements with mathematics in the past have not been positive and have not left him with a sense that he welcomes a mathematical challenge.

Note that we blame neither Eduardo nor his teachers. These short video clips do not carry any of the context that enables us to understand the circumstances surrounding Eduardo's mathematical experiences. Instead, the clips enable us to observe students and consider the kind of experiences they have had that have led them to where they are and to consider the kinds of experiences they would need to have to help them engage more productively with mathematics.

Many other video clips in this collection show students who seem to have productive dispositions toward mathematics, and one way to quickly find some of these is to search for "exceptional reasoning" under the Miscellaneous category. Consider, for example, Felisha, for whom three video clips are listed under Exceptional Reasoning, two for Felisha as a second grader (Video Clips #329 and #330) and one as a fourth grader (Video Clip #325), or one for Conner (Video Clip #132), a first grader. Felisha's and Conner's demeanors seem to reflect children for whom mathematics in particular, and life in general, make sense, and one cannot help but smile when watching them engage. (We like to say that watching children make sense of mathematics makes our hearts sing, and students like Felisha, Conner, Johanna, and Gilberto certainly bring mathematical music to the world!)

Finally, consider one of our favorite video clips, Rachel, a fifth grader (Video Clip #367). The story of Rachel is told in Story #3, the story about conceptual and procedural understanding. We include only one short video clip here.

Before Viewing Video Clip #367 (Rachel, Grade 5, 1:20).

> You are about to view a video of Rachel, a fifth grader. Rachel's teacher usually approached mathematics from a meaning-making perspective, but she was asked to teach a fraction lesson using a state-adopted textbook that approached the topic procedurally, without drawing connections to the concepts. (We refer to this lesson as procedure-only.) After the lesson, students from the class were interviewed, and this video clip was selected from Rachel's interview.
>
> Note that although this video was taken in Southern California, Rachel is not from Hollywood; she is not an actress who is reading a script. She is simply an articulate child speaking for herself.

Analysis.   Although Rachel is remarkable for her ability to draw distinctions between the lesson she was taught "this time" and the typical, more conceptual lessons to which she had grown accustomed, we consider her a typical child in terms of the effect the procedural-only lesson had on her learning. Rachel did not remember the procedure. But more noteworthy was Rachel's explanation for why she did not remember. She said, "We did this before. But I don't exactly remember it as well, because I didn't figure it out for myself." When the interviewer asked Rachel to elaborate, she said, "Well, when she [the teacher] like tells us the answer to something, then I try and find out how she got it. And so when I figure that out, it's easier. And, umm . . . and once I figure it out, it's . . . it stays there, because I was the one who brought it there. So . . . and it's just easier to do, when you figure it out yourself." Notice Rachel's body movements: She used her hands to point to her head and to her stomach, as if knowing resides in one's mind, but also in one's gut. Rachel clearly knew what she knew and knew what she did not know. Rachel also reflects a child who, although she was confused about this problem, is not defined by this temporary confusion. Her confidence in learning was undeterred by this temporary, but mysterious, pedagogical setback. She explained it, but she was not defined by it. Rachel is a lovely example of a child holding productive disposition toward mathematics.

STORY 5, Part IV

Strategic competence: What to do when you don't know what to do.

Strategic competence, defined as the ability to formulate mathematical problems, represent them, and solve them, encompasses what we generally think of as mathematical problem solving. One definition of problem solving is "what one does when one does not know what to do." This definition precludes most of what takes place in U.S. mathematics classrooms from being considered problem solving: Students are shown a technique for solving a particular type of problem and then they practice the technique (Hiebert, Stigler, Jacobs, Givvin, Garnier, Smith, et al., 2005). Although these tasks might be problems if presented in other contexts, they are not problems for students if the students have just been shown what approach to use to solve the tasks. For example, if a mathematics lesson on fraction multiplication contains many multiplication exercises followed by real-life story problems, and if the story problems all contain two fractions that are to be multiplied, students may correctly answer the questions without even reading the story. Any task that a teacher presents as a problem but that the students have just been shown a way to solve is a pseudoproblem. (Compare pseudoproblems to the case of Felisha in Video Clip #325, wherein she was engaged with fraction multiplication even though the task was not presented as such, and she was able to reason through the diagram to arrive at a meaningful solution. Instead of starting with a technique that she was supposed to apply, Felisha applied her conceptual understanding to make sense of a novel situation, and she justified her reasoning by explaining what she did and why what she did made sense.)

Because problem solving is contextually based, we turn to a classroom video clip in which the context is explicit to demonstrate strategic competence.

Before Viewing Video Clip #511 (Jen's Class, Grade 1, 7:27)

You are about to watch a class of first graders working on the following task:

Mrs. Kick had 4 seed packets. Each packet contains 11 seeds. How many seeds did she have in all?

What would you take as evidence that this task is *not* a problem for the children? What would you take as evidence that this task *is* a problem for the children?

While you watch the video clip, look for examples or nonexamples of each of the five strands of mathematical proficiency.

After Viewing Video Clip #511 (Jen's Class, Grade 1, 7:27)

If you apply the definition of *problem solving* as what one does when one does not know what to do, what evidence did you see that this task was a problem for students in this class? Did you observe anyone for whom this task might not have been a problem?

Did you observe other strands of mathematical proficiency in this video clip? What did you take as evidence for each of these other strands?

Early in the video, before students presented solutions to the class, two students using manipulatives argued about whether the seed packets should be represented. What strands of mathematical proficiency were evident during their disagreement?

Ms. Kick asks students if they have any questions or compliments. What was the compliment offered by the first student to offer a compliment? How might this comment relate to productive disposition?

Ms. Kick is teaching 1st grade. Are there grade levels or mathematical subjects for which the approach taken by Ms. Kick would not be successful?

Analysis. This video clip captures many of the strands of mathematical proficiency and, perhaps more important, the connections between and among the strands. Students are shown making sense; they justified their reasoning; they recognized and called attention to, with commendation, noteworthy reasoning; they grappled with a task for which they had no clear solution path, but they were confident that they could make progress, and they selected the tools that they thought would help them make progress down their mathematical path. The mathematical music is loud and clear in this video clip.

Note, too, the teacher's role. From the way she introduced the task to the students, to the independence she granted to students to select tools, to the way she orchestrated the whole class sharing of solutions, the teacher was trying to empower her students to develop all five strands of mathematical proficiency.

STORY 6
Introduction to Interviewing

Teachers can learn a great deal by attending to their students' mathematical thinking, and we have found that even experienced teachers are often surprised to learn how their students are reasoning. The purpose of this story is to help prepare prospective and practicing teachers to conduct a student interview. The focus of this story will be primary-grade (K–2) children's problem solving and understanding of whole number concepts and operations. We hope that, in the process of learning to interview around these tasks, teachers and prospective teachers will develop skills that apply to other mathematical content and to children at other grade levels. (Note that the *Instructor Interview Guide* in the Resources section of the Searchable IMAP Video Collection has additional suggestions for ways to support novices in conducting problem-solving interviews with children. Among the Resources are interview protocols related to early number, decimals, and fractions.)

When prospective and practicing teachers come to see that children are able to solve problems they have not been taught to solve and that children solve problems in ways different from the ways they as adults would solve them, they come to respect children's thinking, and teachers may eventually base their instruction on learning about and responding to their students' thinking to extend the children's learning. Teachers are often amazed at the level of problems young children are capable of solving.

Primary-grade children have a great deal of mathematical knowledge that they have not been taught in school. Children's problem solutions often differ from adults' solutions. For example, young children may solve the problem *Jack had 6 marbles. How many more marbles does Jack need to buy to have 13 altogether?* (which can be represented with the number sentence $6 + ? = 13$) by counting on from 6 to 13 whereas most adults would simply subtract 6 from 13. Because research has shown that children's solution strategies are developmental and that children initially solve problems by directly modeling the quantities in the problem, we ask interviewers to provide counters for children to use as they choose. Further, specific aspects of a problem, such as the location of the unknown quantity (starting quantity, change, resulting quantity) in the problem or the presence of action, affect the child's ability to solve the problem.

By posing problems to a child and stepping back, one can determine the sorts of problems a child is ready to solve, the strategies the child uses, and the numbers with which the child is comfortable. A teacher who understands the research-based hierarchy of problem strategies and problem types, when armed with information gleaned during interviews and instruction, is prepared to extend the child's mathematical thinking by encouraging next steps along the developmental trajectory.

We designed a Children's Mathematical Thinking Experience (CMTE) in which prospective teachers interview K–5 students and come to recognize the need to learn at a deeper level the mathematics they think they know. A student explaining the value of the just-completed CMTE in which she had interviewed children of various grade levels on specific mathematics topics validated our having prospective teachers conduct the interviews to motivate them to engage more fully in mathematics content courses designed for them:

> For people who are going to take [the first mathematics class]—just because *a lot* of the times in class . . . people get *so* mad and *so* frustrated as to why they are learning what they are learning. And then you come [to the CMTE], and you see a kid do exactly what you are learning in [the mathematics] class. And it just makes sense, and it eliminates that whole frustration of feeling like "Why am I learning this? Where am I going to ever use this?" So by taking this class, you *see* how . . . the children actually apply what you are learning, the different styles or the different methods for solving problems.

Materials (Included in Word Files in Resources on Searchable Set of Video Clips)

Materials that relate to interviewing are included in the Resources of the Searchable Video Clips. Four items relate specifically to the Early-Number Interview. Other sets of interview items are provided for interviews related to place value and fractions.

Materials Related to Early-Number Interview

Interview Guide.   This guide for the facilitator details the steps we find useful in preparing inexperienced prospective interviewers to conduct an interview. Issues raised in this guide are included in Part I of this story.

Primary What-Ifs.   These common interview situations are used for discussion or role playing by prospective interviewers in preparing to conduct an interview. These items for discussion of responding to children during an interview are included in Part II of this story.

Early-Number Interview.   We use the Early-Number Interview with children in Grades 1 and 2. In Parts II and III of this story, we include video clips of children solving problems from this interview to raise issues of relative problem difficulty and to show solution strategies one is likely to see children use.

Interview Write-Up.   We use this assignment to help interviewers analyze their interviews so that they can interpret the child's responses and better understand the child's thinking. This assignment is included in Part IV of this story.

Other Sets of Interview Questions

Place Value.   Our students conduct two interviews with third graders: In Place-Value Interview 1 they learn about the child's place-value understanding; they pursue some ideas in greater depth in Place-Value Interview 2.

Rational Number.   Our students conduct several interviews on rational number. Each student pair works with the same fifth grader for all interviews on rational numbers. They first use the Fraction Assessment to find out how the child thinks about fractions. They often use equal-sharing (Empson, 1995) tasks, which we have found to be excellent tasks for raising multiple-representations (Lesh, Post, & Behr, 1987) issues about partitioning, equal-sized pieces, naming fractions, and equivalence. However, even a small number of tasks may be time consuming when the interviewer directs the child toward these many issues. Interviews could be constructed from tasks in the Equal-Sharing Tasks 1 and 2 documents.

Preparing Prospective Interviewers

This purpose of this story is to help prepare prospective or practicing teachers to conduct a student interview. The story is designed to prepare the prospective interviewer to deal with three aspects of any interview: (a) preparing to conduct the interview by considering the interview purpose and how to set at ease the child to be interviewed, (b) considering how to conduct further questioning after a child responds to learn more about the child's thinking, and (c) strategically selecting problems to include and omit during the interview on the basis of a child's thinking. Below we highlight these three aspects of an interview with examples from an early-number interview. We contend, however, that these issues are relevant to any interview and that these suggestions for an early-number interview could be adapted for use with other interviews included in the Resources or devised by the interviewer.

STORY 6, Outline

> **Part I.** Introducing the Interview to the Prospective Interviewer
> (2 video clips)
>
> **Part II.** Activities to Prepare Interviewers for Responding to a Child's Thinking
>
> **Part III.** Decisions One Makes During the Interview
>
> **Part IV.** Analyzing the Interview and Interpreting the Results

STORY 6, Part I

Introducing the interview to the prospective interviewer (purposes for interviewing).

Children have a great deal of mathematical knowledge that they have not been taught in school. The purpose for interviewing a child is to understand how the child thinks, so the stance we suggest is not to teach the child mathematics generally or to solve particular problems but to learn how the child thinks about the problems posed, to determine what sorts of problems the child is able to solve, the number sizes with which the child can work, and solution strategies the child uses so that one is poised to extend the child's thinking. We therefore suggest that interviewers pose problems and listen to the child's response and that they ask questions to clarify the child's thinking, not to direct the child to their ways of thinking about or solving the problem. What do we reward with praise if the answers are not our focus? We show that we value a child's effort and explanation of thinking more than answers.

Story 6, Part I, Clip 1

Before Viewing Video Clip #605 (Interview Introduction, 1:27)

What considerations are important for preparing the child for an interview? [Make brief list.]

In the clip you will watch, attend to how the interviewer explains to the child what she might expect in the upcoming interview.

Discuss considerations that are important for preparing the child for an interview, assuming that the necessary permissions for interviewing the child have been obtained: (a) setting the child at ease; (b) explaining to the child that he may solve problems however he would like and that he will be asked to explain his thinking; (c) explaining that some problems will be difficult and others will be easy, and so the child should not be concerned if he is unable to answer all the questions correctly.

Construct with the prospective interviewers an interview-materials checklist, including the interview questions, paper for the child's use and for the interviewer's notes, an extra pen or pencil, appropriate manipulatives or counters, and a tape recorder and tape.

After Viewing Video Clip #605 (Interview Introduction, 1:27)

What did the interviewer do?

Discuss the features included in the Interview Introduction below, from the Early-Number Interview protocol included in the Resources.

Interview Introduction

- Set the child at ease: Ask child's name, introduce yourself, and so forth.

- Explain that this interview is an assignment for your class. Tell the child that this work will not be graded.

- Explain, "Some questions will be easy, some hard. You are not expected to get them all correct. That's okay. Just do the best you can."

- You are interested in how the child thinks, not in how many problems the child answers correctly. Throughout, you will be asking, "How did you get this?" or "What were you thinking?" Explain to the child that when you ask such questions, you do not mean that the child is wrong; you only want to understand how the child is thinking.

• Introduce the materials: counters, paper and pencil, fingers, any others you use. Tell the child to use whatever he or she wishes.

• Explain why you want to tape the interview and ask for permission. Ask the child's age, names and ages of brothers and sisters, names of best friends, favorite things to do, and so on. You will incorporate this information in the problems you pose. Use the family members' and friends' names in the blanks in the problems, and change the problem contexts to reflect the child's interests.

Remember,
  Set a friendly tone.
  Pay close attention to how the child feels, what the child is thinking and doing.
  Take copious notes on both child and interviewer.
  Consider wait time (you may be uncomfortable with silence, but the child may not be).
  Do not assume that the child wants a question repeated; ask.

STORY 6, Part I, Clip 2

Before Viewing Video Clip #606 (Interview Introduction, 3:41)

In the clip you will watch, an experienced interviewer interviews a second-grade child. The clip will be paused several times for discussion of the interviewer's moves and questions. Consider his reasons for each of these.

Pause While Viewing Video Clip #606 (Interview Introduction, 3:41) to Discuss the Interviewer's Moves

Pause at 0:18. What is the interviewer doing to make Nicole feel at ease? [Consider his intonation. He is not writing notes but is looking at her, showing interest in what she says.]

Pause at 1:16. The interviewer's question ("just you and your brother?") may sound silly, but why did he ask it? [He assumes that she lives with adults, but he does not know whether they are her parents. Because he will pose questions using an adult as a person in the story problem, he needs to know a little about the adults in Nicole's life.]

Pause at 1:37. She had named two things she likes to play. Why does the interviewer ask for a third? [He wants her to name an interest that is easy to use in a word problem. Writing a story problem for 5 + 3 with stones or marbles is easier than with treasure hunts or hide-and-go-seek.]

Pause at 2:18. Nicole has counted to 12. How far should the interviewer have her continue? [If a child is not counting slowly, we suggest having the child count to 31 to show the decade transitions.]

Pause at 2:40. Why did the interviewer ask, "What comes after 8? 19?" even though she had just counted beyond these numbers?
[One can count in different ways. Consider, what letter comes next in the alphabet after R? (S) What letter comes before J? (I). How about 3 before Q? (N). For children learning to count, such questions about numbers can be as difficult as these questions about letters can be for you.]

Pause at 3:14. Nicole was counting by 2s but became confused at 12. What are some options for what the interviewer might say to her at this point? [The interviewer was not interested in correcting Nicole's counting at this time. He wanted to learn about her mathematical thinking, and these responses helped him learn.]

End of Clip. Suppose that when an interviewer asked a child to count by 2s or 5s, the child merely looked at the interviewer? What are some options for the interviewer's next move? [The interviewer might start counting to see whether the child then begins to count along and continues alone.]

STORY 6, Part II

Activities to prepare interviewers to respond to a child's thinking (What-Ifs and 1 Video Clip).

STORY 6, Part II, Activity 1

Following are common children's responses to consider before you conduct the Early-Number Interview. Possible reactions to the responses are given, but they are merely suggestions. Discuss these and other child responses you expect participants to encounter with possible responses designed to gain more information about the child's thinking.

In the dialogues, *C* is the child; *I* is you, the interviewer.

1. You ask the child if he can count by 5s. The child says "No."

   You might begin the count: 5, 10, 15, ... to ensure that the question is clear to the child.

2. You pose the problem "Eva had 6 books; her mother gave her 7 more. How many did she have then?"
   Child says, after a moment, "Thirteen."

   You might ask, "How did you think about that?"

3. You pose the problem "Eva had 6 books; her mother gave her 7 more. How many did she have then?"
Child says nothing, does nothing.

To determine to what the child is attending, you might ask the child, "Can you tell me what the question is?"

4. You pose the problem "Eva had 6 books; her mother gave her 7 more. How many did she have then?"
Child says, after a moment, "Thirteen."
 I: How did you get that?
 C: I did it in my head.

You might ask, "Can you tell me how you were thinking in your head?"

5. You pose the problem "Eva had 6 books; her mother gave her 7 more. How many did she have then?"
Child counts out 6 blocks then counts out 7 more and puts them together with the first 6. Counts all the blocks, beginning with 1, 2, 3, . . . ; miscounts; says, "Twelve."

In this case, you may decide to do nothing; although the child's answer is incorrect, you have learned how the child was thinking.

6. You pose the problem "Eva had 6 books; her mother gave her 7 more. How many did she have then?"
Child says, after a moment, "Thirteen."
 I: What did you do?
 C: I did it in my head.
 I: How did you think about it?
 C: I counted.

Ask, "Can you tell me how you counted?"

7. You pose the problem "Eva had 6 books; her mother gave her 7 more. How many did she have then?"
Child says nothing, does nothing.
 I: Could you use the blocks to help you solve the problem?
Child counts out 6 blocks and stops. Long pause.

To determine whether the child remembers the problem context, point to the six blocks and ask, "So, what are these?" Pause. "What do they stand for in the problem?" Pause. If necessary, ask, "Are they children? Books?"

8. You pose the problem "Eva had 6 books; her mother gave her 7 more. How many did she have then?"
Child counts out 6 blocks then counts out 7 more. With the 6 in one group, child begins counting the 7 in the other group by saying, "6, 7, 8, 9, 10, 11, 12."

Because the fundamental purpose of interviewing is to learn about the child's thinking and not to correct errors and because the thinking in this solution is clear, we might not follow-up with any questions.

STORY 6, Part II, Clip 1

Interviewers make decisions throughout an interview about which questions to pose, when to respond to a child's thinking, when to move on, and so on. Video Clip #607 shows a child responding to several story problems from the Early Number interview. We ask students to attend to which problems the child could solve and which he could not and to his solution strategies—topics discussed in more detail in Part III of this story. This clip highlights several issues including wait time, a child who might have special needs, and a child who is somewhat surprising in the problems he is and is not able to solve.

Before Viewing Video Clip #607 (Richard, Grade 2, 8:13)

In the video clip you will view, an experienced interviewer posed the following problems to a second grader, early in the school year. Which problems would you expect him to solve with ease? Which problems might be more difficult for him? How would you expect him to solve each problem?

Richard has 4 toy cars. Cameron gives you 12 more toy cars. How many toy cars do you have now?

Richard has 14 toy cars. He gives 5 toy cars to Cameron. How many toy cars does Richard have left?

Richard, suppose you had 6 marbles. How many more marbles would you need to buy to have 13 altogether?

A pack of gum has 5 pieces in it. How many pieces of gum would I have, if I had three packs of gum?

After Viewing Video Clip #607 (Richard, Grade 2, 8:13)

Describe Richard's solution attempt for each problem.

What surprised you in Richard's interview?

Do you expect that in a classroom, Richard had the opportunity to solve problems that required the time and effort he expended on the marbles problem?

Note that additional problems from the Prob 607 problem file could be posed.

Analysis. Richard used blocks to model the quantities in each problem directly. He miscounted in solving the first two problems and, after much effort, solved the third problem. As many children do, he solved the gum problem without difficulty by modeling 5 sticks from one pack of gum with blocks and counting the 5 sticks in each of the remaining two packs on his fingers. In solving the first two problems, Richard miscounted, but the interviewer saw that he had correctly modeled the problem and understood how to solve it. He focused on Richard's thinking about the problem, not on his answers resulting from a miscount. The interviewer gave Richard much time and support to solve the third problem; Richard spent 3:30 solving that problem, probably the reason the interviewer did ask him to recount to get the correct answer when Richard first counted 8 instead of 7. Usually when Richard asked for clarification of the quantities in the problem, the interviewer repeated the entire problem to avoid breaking up the problem, but occasionally he simply answered Richard's question about a quantity Richard forgot.

Richard's responses are surprising in that he incorrectly answered the first two problems, considered to be easiest in terms of their problem structures because the quantities can be modeled directly and in both contexts, one joining and one separating, the result of the action stated in the problem is the unknown. In the marbles problem, the interviewer's patience in repeating the problem for Richard was rewarded in that Richard persevered and solved this problem that has a structure more challenging than that of the first two problems because he needed to find the amount of change between the starting and ending quantities. Richard showed that he understood the problem to be solved in all four cases.

STORY 6, Part III

Problem-selection decisions one makes during the interview on the basis of a child's responses (excerpts from multiple video clips).

During the interview, the interviewer will decide which questions to pose and which to omit from the interview protocol, which answers to probe, and, perhaps, additional questions to pose to investigate a conjecture about a child's thinking. To prepare the interviewer to make such decisions, video clips are selected to highlight the relative difficulties of the problems, strategies students commonly use to solve these problems, and ways children may think about the problems. These clips show direct modeling, counting, derived-fact, and recall strategies.

For homework preceding the interview, we give the prospective interviewers copies of the interview questions and often ask them to predict whether and how a child will answer some of the questions. In doing so, they become familiar with the interview questions and better able to notice the relevant features of a child's solution.

Suggested reading for this activity is an article from *Teaching Children Mathematics,* "Making the most of story problems" (Jacobs & Ambrose, 2008).

A. Using Direct Modeling and Counting Strategies to Solve Problems

Young children, before they learn addition and subtraction facts or hear about operations such as addition and subtraction, can model the situation in a story problem with counters of various kinds, including fingers, and perform the actions in the problem with the counters to solve the problem.

Before Showing Video Clips of Children Using Modeling and Counting Strategies

You are about to watch children solve problems by directly modeling the quantities in the problem and counting all or by counting in other ways. Consider the differences in the ways children solve these problems.

In what ways might a child use modeling and counting to solve *Eric has five apples, and his mother gives him three more apples. How many apples does Eric have now?*

How would you expect a child to count to solve *Eric has 4 toy cars. And his friend gave him 7 more toy cars. So how many cars does Eric have now?*

Show Video Clips of Children Using Modeling and Counting Strategies

Discuss differences in children's counting strategies in the videos.

Direct modeling, counting all

(Video #117—0:00–0:55) An experienced interviewer posed *Eric has five apples, and his mother gives him three more apples. How many apples does Eric have now?* Arlene directly modeled both numbers and counted all.

(Video #120—0:00–1:14) A prospective teacher posed *Trina has 6 marbles. How many marbles does Trina need to buy to have 13?* Arriel counted 6, counted on to 14, and counted the 8 she added on. She correctly solved $6 + ? = 14$ by counting all. She then solved the original problem in a similar way. One might accept the solution for the problem Arriel solved first because she showed her thinking on the type of problem posed. Or one might pose the original problem again to determine whether Arriel would simply adjust her solution or begin again to solve the problem.

Counting on from larger when larger number is first.

(Video #193—0:33–1:04) A prospective teacher posed *There are eight boys and five girls in the room. How many children are in the room altogether?*

Trina explained that she put the 8 in her head and counted on 5 more from 8. She counted on from the larger number, but because it was the first number mentioned in the problem, one cannot tell whether she did so to use a more efficient strategy than counting on from 5.

Counting on from larger when larger number is second in the problem

(**Video #165—0:00–0:55**) An experienced interviewer posed *Eric has 4 toy cars. And his friend gave him 7 more toy cars. So how many cars does Eric have now?* After considerable wait time, Jocelyn explained that she counted on from 7. That is, she counted on from the larger number even though the larger number was not the number of cars Eric had to start the problem. Her strategy was more efficient than directly modeling the action in the problem.

(**Video #115—0:00–0:42**) An experienced interviewer posed *Eric has 4 toy cars, and his friend gave him 7 more toy cars. How many cars does Eric have now?* Anjzanice explained that she counted on "from the larger number."

B. Using Derived Facts to Solve Problems

As shown in the preceding set of video clips, children can solve problems before memorizing facts by using modeling and counting strategies. The next level of sophistication in children's strategies is use of facts that they derive from facts that they have memorized. The facts memorized are often doubles or facts that make 10. The children use these facts to add or subtract to get to the number they need to solve the problem.

Before Showing Video Clips of Children Using Derived-Facts Strategies

In the clips you will watch, children use addition facts they know to solve problems involving facts they do not know.

How might a child use a known doubles fact to solve the following problem?

Jill had 6 Beanie Babies. How many more does she need to collect to have 13 Beanie Babies altogether?

How might a child use a known fact for making 10 to solve the following problem?

Let's say that Breanna S. has 4 Pokemon cards, and her friend gives her 7 more Pokemon cards. How many Pokemon cards does she have altogether?

Show Video Clips of Children Using Derived-Facts Strategies

(Video #134—0:00–0:27) An experienced interviewer poses *Jill had 6 Beanie Babies. How many more does she need to collect to have 13 Beanie Babies altogether?* Connor explains that he knows that the answer is 7 because 6 + 6 = 12 and 1 more is 13.

(Video #128—0:00–1:22) An experienced interviewer poses *Let's say that Breanna S. has 4 Pokemon cards, and her friend gives her 7 more Pokemon cards. How many Pokemon cards does she have altogether?* Cheyenne self-corrects while explaining, using 3 + 7 = 10 and 1 more is 11.

C. Using Recalled Facts to Solve Problems

Through solving problems using their own strategies, children come to memorize addition and subtraction facts and some problems are difficult to solve without recalling facts. If one knows the start and change quantities (Result Unknown), the problem can be modeled with the quantities joined or separated to find the result. If one knows the start quantity and the result (Change Unknown), one can count up or down from the start to the result and then count the amount added or taken away. However, if one does not know the start quantity (Start Unknown), modeling the problem is difficult. Children can employ other sophisticated thinking to solve such problems before they memorize facts, but in our only examples of successfully solved Start Unknown problems (Clips 110 and 119), the children used their known fact 5 + 4 = 9 to solve ? + 4 = 9.

**Before Showing Video Clips of Start-Unknown Problems
Solved Using Recall**

How might a child who uses modeling to solve problems model the following two problems?

You have some toy scooters. You go to the store, and you buy four more. And now you have nine scooters. How many did you have to start with?

Suppose you had some toy cars, and you went to the store, and you bought four more toy cars. And then you had nine toy cars altogether. How many toy cars did you have to start with?

Knowing what addition fact would help children solve these problems?

Show Video Clips of Start-Unknown Problems Solved Using Recall

> **(Video #110, 0:00–0:36)** A prospective teacher posed the problem *You have some toy scooters. You go to the store, and you buy four more. And now you have nine scooters. How many did you have to start with?* Andrew knows that 5 + 4 = 9 so he "had to start with 5."
>
> **(Video #119, 0:00–1:53)** An experienced interviewer posed the problem *Arriel, suppose you had some toy cars, and you went to the store, and you bought four more toy cars. And then you had nine toy cars altogether. How many toy cars did you have to start with?* Arriel knows that 4 + 5 = 9.
>
> Do you think that she needed to use the cubes? What is your evidence for your answer? Notice that she first counted the 5 cubes, then the 4.

STORY 6, Part IV

Analyzing the interview and interpreting the results (interview write-up).

We include a copy of our interview write-up assignment, which you may adapt as needed. Note that we refer to a partner in the assignment. Because of circumstances available to us, we teach some courses on site at local elementary schools, and we often interview children drawn from the same class. We place our prospective elementary school teachers in pairs when they interview one child; one student leads the interview while the other student takes notes but may interject on occasion. We often loan the students tape recorders to audiotape the interview to allow for deeper reflection on the interview. If your participants arrange and conduct their interviews on their own time and work alone, we recommend that they audiotape the interviews.

Interview Write-Up

After each interview, write a review of the interview you or your partner conducted. The review should contain the following information:

A. General information
  - your name and the name of your partner,
  - the age and grade of the student you interviewed,
  - any pertinent information you would like to share about the child, and
  - all the questions you asked (placed in an appendix).

B. Your analysis

  Throughout your analysis, keep in mind the following general questions:

  1. What did you learn about the child?
  2. What did you learn about the child's mathematical thinking?
  3. What did you learn about mathematics?

To help you answer these general questions, choose 3 or 4 interview items to analyze in depth and explain your problem choice. (Ask yourself, "Which questions helped me learn most about the child's thinking?") State the problems and describe the child's strategies. In your analysis you may want to consider some of the following issues:

- what you learned about the challenges of mathematics teaching and learning;

- what you learned that relates to your experiences in your mathematics course;

- how the availability or lack of manipulatives affected the interview;

- what you learned about the interviewers (that is, yourself and your partner);

- what you thought went well and what did not go so well;

- what you would do differently if you were able to conduct this interview again;

- what you would do next if you were this child's teacher;

- anything that surprised you.

If your analysis is long and integrated, you may focus on fewer problems. The purpose for the assignment is to have you be as thoughtful as possible about what you could learn from the interview.

A Caution About Your Write-Ups

Please do not include an assessment of the child's overall personality (*e.g.*, happy, self-confident, or nervous child) or overall ability level (*e.g.*, smart or slow child), because those statements do not provide useful information for our purposes. You may want to comment on a child's performance in solving a particular problem (*e.g.*, child was very confident with her solution strategy to problem *x*), but please avoid generalities, inasmuch as you will meet with each child for only a limited time.

Grading

Your work will be evaluated on the thoughtfulness of your comments—not on the expertise of your interviewing! So have fun and experiment!

References Cited and Other Sources

Ball, D. L. (1993). Halves, pieces, and twoths: Constructing and using representational contexts in teaching fractions. In T. P. Carpenter, E. Fennema, & T. A. Romberg (Eds.), *Rational numbers: An integration of research* (pp. 157–196). Hillsdale, NJ: Erlbaum.

Ball, D. L., Lubienski, S. T., & Mewborn, D. S. (2001). Research on teaching mathematics: The unsolved problem of teachers' mathematical knowledge. In V. Richardson (Ed.), *Handbook of research on teaching* (4th ed., pp. 433–456). Washington, DC: American Educational Research Association.

Ball, D. L., Hill, H. H., & Bass, H. (2005). Knowing mathematics for teaching: Who knows mathematics well enough to teach third grade, and how can we decide? *American Mathematical Educator,* Fall, 14–46.

Carpenter, T. P., Ansell, E., Franke, M. L., Fennema, E., & Weisbeck, L. (1993). Models of problem solving: A study of kindergarten children's problem-solving processes. *Journal for Research in Mathematics Education, 24,* 427–440.

Carpenter, T. P., Corbitt, M. K., Kepner, H., Lindquist, M. M., & Reys, R. E. (1980). Results and implications of the Second NAEP Mathematics Assessment: Elementary school. *Arithmetic Teacher, 27*(8), 10–12, 44–47.

Carpenter, T. P., Fennema, E., Franke, M. L., Levi, L., & Empson, S. (1999). *Children's mathematics: Cognitively guided instruction.* Portsmouth, NH: Heinemann.

Carpenter, T. P., & Moser, J. M. (1984). The acquisition of addition and subtraction concepts in grades one through three. *Journal for Research in Mathematics Education, 15*(3), 179–202.

Clement, L. (2004). A model for understanding, using, and connecting representations. *Teaching Children Mathematics, 11,* 97–102.

Cochran-Smith, M., & Lytle, S. (1999). Relationships of knowledge and practice: Teacher learning in communities. In A. Iran-Nejad & P. D. Pearson (Eds.), *Review of research in education* (Vol. 24, pp. 249–306). Washington, DC: American Educational Research Association.

Cochran-Smith, M., & Lytle, S. L. (2001). Beyond certainty: Taking an inquiry stance on practice. In A. Lieberman & L. Miller (Eds.), *Teachers caught in the action: Professional development that matters* (45–58). Teachers College Press: New York.

Empson, S. B. (1995). Using sharing situations to help children learn fractions. *Teaching Children Mathematics,* 110–114.

Empson, S., & Levi, L. (in press). *Extending children's mathematics: Fractions and decimals.* Portsmouth, NH: Heinemann.

Fuson, K. C., Wearne, D. H., Hiebert, J. C., Murray, H. G., Human, P. G., Olivier, A. I., Carpenter, T. P., & Fennema, E. (1997). Children's conceptual structures for multidigit numbers and methods of multidigit addition and subtraction. *Journal for Research in Mathematics Education, 28,* 130–162.

Hiebert, J., & Carpenter, T. P. (1992). Learning and teaching with understanding. In D. A. Grouws (Ed.), *Handbook of research on mathematics teaching and learning* (pp. 65–97). New York: Macmillan.

Hiebert, J., Stigler, W., Jacobs, J. K., Givvin, K. B., Garnier, H., Smith, M., et al. (2005). Mathematics teaching in the United States today (and tomorrow): Results from the TIMSS 1999 video study. *Educational Evaluation and Policy Analysis, 27,* 111–132.

Hiebert, J., & Wearne, D. (1992). Links between teaching and learning place value with understanding in first grade. *Journal for Research in Mathematics Education, 23,* 98–122.

Jacobs, V. R., & Ambrose, R. C. (2008). Making the most of story problems. *Teaching Children Mathematics, 15,* 260–266.

Jacobs, V. R., Ambrose, R. C., Clement, L., & Brown, D. (2006). Using teacher-produced videotapes of student interviews as discussion catalysts. *Teaching Children Mathematics, 12,* 276–281.

Jacobs, V. R., & Kusiak, J. (2006). Got tools? Exploring children's use of math tools during problem solving. *Teaching Children Mathematics, 12*, 470–477.

Jacobs, V. R., Lamb, L. C., & Philipp, R. A. (2010). Professional noticing of children's mathematical thinking. *Journal for Research in Mathematics Education, 41*, 169–202.

Jacobs, V. R., & Philipp R. A. (2004). Mathematical thinking: Helping prospective and practicing teachers focus. *Teaching Children Mathematics*, 11, 194–201.

Jacobs, V. R., & Philipp, R. A. (2010). Supporting children during problem solving. *Teaching Children Mathematics. 17*(2), 98–105.

Kamii, C. (1986). Place value: An explanation of its difficulty and educational implications for the primary grades. *Journal of Research in Childhood Education, 1*, 75–86.

Lamb, L. C., Philipp, R. A., Jacobs, V. R., & Schappelle, B. P. (2009). Developing teachers' stances of inquiry: Studying teachers' evolving perspectives. In D. Slavit, T. H. Nelson, & A. Kennedy (Eds.), *Perspectives on supported collaborative teacher inquiry* (pp. 16–45). New York: Routledge.

Lesh, R., Post, T., & Behr, M. (1987). Representations and translations among representations in mathematics learning and problem solving. In C. Janvier (Ed.), *Problems of representation in the teaching and learning of mathematics* (pp. 33–40). Hillsdale, NJ: Erlbaum.

Ma, L. (1999). *Knowing and teaching elementary mathematics: Teachers' understanding of fundamental mathematics in China and the United States*. Mahwah, NJ: Erlbaum.

Mack, N. K. (1990). Learning fractions with understanding: Building on informal knowledge. *Journal for Research in Mathematics Education, 21*, 16–32.

Mason, J. (2011). Noticing: Roots and branches. In M. G., Sherin, V. R. Jacobs, & R. A. Philipp (Eds.), *Mathematics teacher noticing: Seeing through teachers' eyes* (pp. 35–50). New York: Routledge.

Moss, J., & Case, R. (1999). Developing children's understanding of the rational numbers: A new model and an experimental curriculum. *Journal for Research in Mathematics Education, 30*, 122–147.

National Center for Education Statistics. (1999). *Highlights from the TIMSS 1999 video study of eighth-grade mathematics teaching*. Washington, DC: National Center for Education Statistics. Retrieved May 12, 2005, from http://nces.ed.gov/pubs2003/timssvideo/

National Council of Teachers of Mathematics. (2000). *Principles and standards for school mathematics*. Reston, VA: Author.

National Research Council. (1999). *How people learn: Brain, mind, experience, and school*. Washington, DC: National Academy Press.

National Research Council. (2001). *Adding it up: Helping children learn mathematics*. Washington, DC: National Academy Press.

Pesek, D. D., & Kirshner, D. (2002). Interference of instrumental instruction in subsequent relational learning. In J. Sowder & B. Schappelle (Eds.), *Lessons learned from research* (pp. 101–107). Reston, VA: National Council of Teachers of Mathematics.

Philipp, R. A. (1996). Multicultural mathematics and alternative algorithms: Using knowledge from many cultures. *Teaching Children Mathematics, 3*, 128–135.

Philipp, R. A. (2000). *Unpacking a conceptual lesson: The case of dividing fractions*. San Diego, CA: Center for Research in Mathematics and Science Education.

Philipp, R. A. (2007). Mathematics teachers' beliefs and affect. In F. K. Lester (Ed.), *Second handbook of research on mathematics teaching and learning* (pp. 257–315). Reston, VA: National Council of Teachers of Mathematics.

Philipp, R. A., & Vincent, C. (2003). Reflecting on learning fractions without understanding. *ON-Math: Online Journal of School Mathematics* (The On-Line Journal of the National Council of Teachers of Mathematics), *2(2)*. [*Note:* A draft of this article, with the draft titled "A fifth-grade student reflecting upon learning fractions without understanding: A video example," can be found at www.sci.sdsu.edu/CRMSE/IMAP/pubs.html.]

Ross, S. H. (1990). Children's acquisition of place-value numeration concepts: The roles of cognitive development and instruction. *Focus on Learning Problems in Mathematics, 12*(1), 1–17.

Sherin, B., & Star, J. (2011). Reflections on the study of teacher noticing. In M. G., Sherin, V. R. Jacobs, & R. A. Philipp (Eds.), *Mathematics teacher noticing: Seeing through teachers' eyes* (pp. 66–78). New York: Routledge.

Sherin, M. G., Jacobs, V. R., & Philipp, R. A. (Eds.). (2011). *Mathematics teacher noticing: Seeing through teachers' eyes.* New York: Routledge.

Shulman, L. S. (1986). Those who understand: Knowledge growth in teaching. *Educational Researcher, 15*(2), 4–14.

Sowder, J. T., Philipp, R. A., Armstrong, B. E., & Schappelle, B. P. (1998). *Middle-grade teachers' mathematical knowledge and its relationship to instruction.* New York: State University of New York Press.

Thompson, A. G., Philipp, R. A., Thompson, P. W., & Boyd, B. A. (1994). Calculational and conceptual orientations in teaching mathematics. In D. B. Aichele & A. F. Coxford (Eds.), *Professional development for teachers of mathematics* (pp. 79–92). Reston, VA: National Council of Teachers of Mathematics.

Thompson, P. W. (1995). Notation, convention, and quantity in elementary mathematics. In J. T. Sowder & B. P. Schappelle (Eds.), *Providing a foundation for teaching mathematics in the middle grades* (pp. 199–221). New York: State University of New York Press.

Tzur, R. (1999). An integrated study of children's construction of improper fractions and the teacher's role in promoting that learning. *Journal for Research in Mathematics Education, 30,* 390–416.

Vincent, C. (2002). *Digging beneath the surface: The power of the interview.* Manuscript submitted for publication.

Wearne, D., & Hiebert, J. (1988). A cognitive approach to meaningful mathematics instruction: Testing a local theory using decimal numbers. *Journal for Research in Mathematics Education, 19,* 371–384.

Wearne, D., & Hiebert, J. (1994). Research into practice: Place value and addition and subtraction. *Arithmetic Teacher, 41,* 272–274.

Wells, G. (1999). *Dialogic inquiry: Toward a sociocultural practice and theory of education.* Cambridge, UK: University Press.

Wilson, S., & Berne, J. (1999). Teacher learning and the acquisition of professional knowledge: An examination of research on contemporary professional development. *Review of Research in Education, 24,* 173–209.

Term	Category	Description of Use
algebra	Content	A pattern or relationship between numbers is recognized or generalized.
comparison	Content	Two quantities, decimal numbers, fractions, or whole numbers, are compared.
counting	Content	Numerals are named in order, or the importance of counting is noted by a teacher.
decimal addition	Content	At least one addend is a decimal amount.
decimals	Content	A decimal number is part of the problem.
decimal subtraction	Content	The minuend, the subtrahend, or both are decimal amounts.
equal sharing	Content	Equal-sized groups are to be formed.
fraction addition	Content	At least one addend is a fractional amount.
fraction division	Content	At least one quantity among the divisor, dividend, and quotient is a fractional amount.
fraction multiplication	Content	At least one factor is a fractional amount.
fractions	Content	A fraction is part of the problem.
fraction subtraction	Content	The minuend, the subtrahend, or both are fractional amounts.
identifying fractions	Content	A fractional amount to be named is represented with a drawing or other representation.
missing addend	Content	One addend and the sum are known. We also label such problems both as whole number addition (children may see them as joining situations) and as whole number subtraction (to adults they may be subtraction problems).
money	Content	Dollars or cents are in the problem context or the solution.
place value	Content	The values of one or more digits in some number in the problem are discussed, or place-value understanding is especially relevant for solving the problem.
renaming fractions	Content	One is asked to convert between mixed numbers and improper fractions, between equivalent fractions, or between fractions and decimals.
role of the unit	Content	Keeping track of the whole is important in the fraction problem posed.
story problem	Content	A problem is presented in a context.
whole number addition	Content	The addends are whole numbers.
whole number division	Content	The dividend and divisor are whole numbers. The quotient may not be an integer.
whole number multiplication	Content	The factors are whole numbers.
whole number subtraction	Content	The minuend and the subtrahend are whole numbers.
composing/decomposing numbers	Strategy	The child breaks apart or puts together numbers in a way other than as they are stated in the problem.
counting back	Strategy	To find a difference or a missing addend, the child counts by ones from the higher number in a problem to a lower number.

Term	Category	Description of Use
counting on	Strategy	To find an answer, a child counts by ones from one number given in the problem.
counting up	Strategy	The child counts using convenient numbers, usually multiples of 10, to find a missing addend.
derived fact	Strategy	The child builds upon a previously known fact to solve a problem (e.g., knows $5 + 5 = 10$, so says $5 + 6 = 11$).
direct modeling	Strategy	The child uses concrete materials or drawings to represent the quantities and the action in the problem.
distributive property	Strategy	The child uses the distributive property, perhaps without being aware of the property name, in his or her solution.
drawing	Strategy	The child draws to represents all or part of the problem.
expanded algorithm	Strategy	The child uses an algorithm that shows partial sums or products and may begin working from the left instead of the right.
fingers	Strategy	The child uses his or her fingers to help solve the problem.
hundred chart	Strategy	The child uses a chart with the numbers 1 to 100, arranged in rows of 10, to solve the problem.
invented strategy	Strategy	We infer that the child is using an appropriate strategy he or she has constructed, or a teacher discusses the value of children's creating their own strategies.
manipulatives	Strategy	The child uses concrete objects to facilitate his or her thinking.
misconception	Strategy	The child expresses an incorrect mathematical idea that is commonly held by children.
misconstrued strategy	Strategy	The child incorrectly applies a learned strategy or devises an inappropriate strategy.
number sense	Strategy	The child demonstrates good understanding of numbers, their relative sizes, and their relationships. Decomposing and re-composing numbers and using place-value ideas to simplify computations are common number-sense strategies.
number sense not evident	Strategy	The child clearly demonstrates a poor understanding of numbers, their sizes, and their relationships.
patterns	Strategy	The child uses pattern recognition in solving a problem.
procedure	Strategy	The child uses a set of steps in manipulating numerals to solve the problem.
recall	Strategy	The child retrieves a memorized fact to solve the problem.
repeated addition	Strategy	The child adds a number n times instead of multiplying the number by n.
skip counting	Strategy	The child counts by, for example, 2s, 5s, or 10s to solve the problem.
standard algorithm	Strategy	The child uses the algorithm most commonly used in the United States.
clarify	Teaching/ Interviewing	The interviewer repeats or rephrases the problem.
conceptual instruction	Teaching/ Interviewing	The child is encouraged to construct mathematical ideas and the relationships between and among those ideas, or teachers discuss the advantages of teaching conceptually.
difficult interview	Teaching/ Interviewing	The interviewer has difficulty eliciting a response or appropriate responses from the child.

Term	Category	Description of Use
extension question	Teaching/ Interviewing	On the basis of a previous response, the interviewer poses a question intended to provide more information about the child's understanding.
in/out of context	Teaching/ Interviewing	Two problems using the same numbers are posed with and without a context.
introducing interview	Teaching/ Interviewing	The beginning of a typical interview is shown.
novice interviewer	Teaching/ Interviewing	A preservice teacher's decision making plays a role in the interview.
probing	Teaching/ Interviewing	The interviewer uses effective secondary questioning to further elicit a child's thinking or solution.
procedural instruction	Teaching/ Interviewing	The steps used in a particular procedure are being taught.
scaffolding	Teaching/ Interviewing	The interviewer uses a question or suggestion or a series of questions or suggestions to support the child's understanding.
small group	Teaching/ Interviewing	Fewer than eight children are being instructed.
student discourse	Teaching/ Interviewing	Children share their mathematical understanding with other children, or a teacher discusses the value of student discourse.
wait time	Teaching/ Interviewing	After posing a question, the interviewer waits during a period of silence while the child seems to be thinking about the problem.
whole class	Teaching/ Interviewing	Instruction takes place within the context of the children in a classroom, or a teacher discusses creating an appropriate classroom environment.
cognitive dissonance	Miscellaneous	The child becomes aware that his or her answer is incorrect, often while explaining the solution or solving the problem a second time.
exceptional reasoning	Miscellaneous	An inventive or exceptional solution is presented by the child.
intermediate	Miscellaneous	The child is in Grades 4–6.
language issue	Miscellaneous	The child's solution to or understanding of the problem is complicated by his or her limited English proficiency.
primary	Miscellaneous	The child is in Grades K–3.
self-corrects	Miscellaneous	After giving an incorrect answer, the child corrects the answer while explaining the solution.
Spanish speaker	Miscellaneous	The child's predominant language is Spanish.
teacher reflection/advice	Miscellaneous	A teacher discusses his or her craft, students, or a particular lesson.
technology	Miscellaneous	A child uses a personal data assistant (PDA) to solve problems.
wrong answer	Miscellaneous	The child responds with an incorrect answer.

APPENDIX B
Complete List and Description of 232 IMAP Clips

CLIP #	TIME	TITLE	DESCRIPTION	GENDER	GRADE	ETHNICITY	CONTENT	TEACHING / INTERVIEWING	STRATEGY	MISC	SCREEN CAPTURE NAME
100	0:54	Ally, 187 + ? = 400	She counts up from 187 by hundreds to get to 387, and knows that she took 200 to get there. Then she adds 10 to 87 to get 97, and then she adds 3 more to get 100. She adds 10 + 3 + 200 = 213.	F	3rd	Caucasian	whole number addition, story problem, missing addend, whole number subtraction, place value		counting up, number sense, composing/decomposing numbers, fingers	primary	none
101	0:21	Ally, 400 − 150	She knows that 400 − 100 = 300 and 300 − 50 = 250.	F	3rd	Caucasian	whole number subtraction, story problem, place value		composing/decomposing numbers, number sense	primary	none
102	0:30	Ally, 6 × 14	She knows that 6 × 10 = 60 and 6 × 4 = 24. So 60 + 24 = 84.	F	3rd	Caucasian	whole number multiplication, story problem		distributive property, number sense	primary, Exceptional Reasoning	none
103	0:28	Amber, value of 32	When asked the value of each numeral in 32, she knows that the 2 is in the one's place and the 3 is in the ten's place.	F	2nd	Caucasian	place value		recall	primary	none
104	1:24	Andrew, 120 + 96	He thinks of the problem as 190 + 26. He adds 190 + 10 and gets 200. Then he adds another 10 to get 210, and then adds 6 and gets 216.	M	2nd	Caucasian	whole number addition, place value	probing	composing/decomposing numbers, invented strategy, number sense	primary, Exceptional Reasoning	0104 at 039.jpg
105	0:52	Andrew, 14 − 5	He thinks that the problem is 14 − 4 and counts back on his fingers to 10. To clarify, interviewer asks how many he gave away.	M	2nd	Caucasian	whole number subtraction, story problem	clarify	counting back, fingers	primary, wrong answer	0105 at 038.jpg
106	1:19	Andrew, 20 ÷ 4	He uses blocks to model this measurement-division problem.	M	2nd	Caucasian	whole number division, story problem		direct modeling, manipulatives	primary	0106 at 115.jpg
107	1:08	Andrew, 274 + 368	He uses an expanded algorithm he has been shown, first adding the hundreds, then the tens, then the ones.	M	2nd	Caucasian	whole number addition, place value		expanded algorithm, procedure, number sense	primary	0107 at 100.jpg

CLIP #	TIME	TITLE	DESCRIPTION	GENDER	GRADE	ETHNICITY	CONTENT	TEACHING / INTERVIEWING	STRATEGY	MISC	SCREEN CAPTURE NAME
108	0:15	Andrew, 5 + 3	He counts on from 5 on his fingers.	M	1st	Caucasian	whole number addition, story problem		counting on, fingers	primary	0108 at 013.jpg
109	0:38	Andrew, 34 + 59	He solves it by first adding the tens, then adding the ones.	M	2nd	Caucasian	whole number addition, place value		composing/decomposing numbers, number sense	primary	none
110	0:36	Andrew, ? + 4 = 9	He just knows that 5 + 4 = 9, so he is able to solve the start-unknown problem.	M	2nd	Caucasian	whole number subtraction, whole number addition, missing addend, story problem		recall	primary	none
111	1:11	Andrew, 47 − 39	He subtracts 30 from 40 and gets 10. He subtracts 7 from 9 and gets 2. Then he subtracts 2 from 10 and gets a final answer of 8.	M	2nd	Caucasian	whole number subtraction, place value	probing	composing/decomposing numbers, invented strategy, number sense	primary, Exceptional Reasoning	none
112	0:53	Andrew, 7 × 12	He knows that 7 × 10 = 70. Using seven fingers, he skip counts by twos to 14. So, 70 + 14 = 84.	M	2nd	Caucasian	whole number multiplication, place value		fingers, distributive property, skip counting, number sense, repeated addition	primary	0112 at 024.jpg
113	0:53	Andrew, part unknown, 8, 14	He counts on from 8 on his fingers.	M	2nd	Caucasian	story problem, whole number addition, whole number subtraction, missing addend		counting on, fingers	primary	none
114	2:28	Anjzanice, 3 × 5	She uses blocks to model but gets a wrong answer.	F	1st	African American	whole number multiplication	difficult interview, scaffolding, clarify	direct modeling, manipulatives, repeated addition	primary, wrong answer	0114 at 227.jpg
115	0:42	Anjzanice, 4 + 7	She keeps 7 in her head and then counts 4 more on her fingers.	F	1st	African American	whole number addition, story problem	probing	counting on, fingers	primary	0115 at 038.jpg
116	2:17	Arlene, 12 − 4	At the interviewer's suggestion, she uses blocks to model the problem. Interviewer facilitates each step.	F	1st	Latino	whole number subtraction, story problem	difficult interview, scaffolding	direct modeling, manipulatives	primary	0116 at 137.jpg
117	0:55	Arlene, 5 + 3	She counts on her fingers, but does not show her fingers until prompted to do so.	F	1st	Latino	whole number addition, story problem	probing	direct modeling, fingers	primary	0117 at 048.jpg

CLIP #	TIME	TITLE	DESCRIPTION	GENDER	GRADE	ETHNICITY	CONTENT	TEACHING / INTERVIEWING	STRATEGY	MISC	SCREEN CAPTURE NAME
118	4:39	Arriel, 18 ÷ 3	She draws the solution to the problem. She uses guess-and-check, first guessing that each person gets 5 M&M's candies, then redrawing and redistributing 6 to each.	F	2nd	African American	whole number division, story problem, equal sharing		drawing, direct modeling	primary	0118 at 356.jpg
119	1:53	Arriel, ? + 4 = 9	She recalls 4 + 5 = 9 but uses blocks to verify her answer for this start-unknown problem.	F	2nd	African American	missing addend, whole number addition, whole number subtraction, story problem	extension question	recall, direct modeling, manipulatives	primary	0119 at 138.jpg
120	2:04	Arriel, 6 + ? = 13	Initially she says that the answer is 8 but has used the wrong number. Interviewer says that she wants 13, not 14. She uses blocks to solve the problem and answers 7.	F	2nd	African American	whole number subtraction, whole number addition, missing addend, story problem	clarify	direct modeling, manipulatives	primary, wrong answer	0120 at 140.jpg
121	0:48	Arriel, part unknown, 8, 14	She counts out 14 blocks. She separates 8 blocks and then counts the rest. She says 6.	F	2nd	African American	story problem, whole number addition, whole number subtraction, missing addend		direct modeling, manipulatives	primary	0121 at 041.jpg
122	2:35	Austin, 20 ÷ 4	He answers 10 cars. Interviewer asks him to show her 20 kids, using the blocks, then to show 4 kids in the car. She facilitates each step. He makes 5 groups of 4 kids.	M	K	Caucasian	whole number division, story problem	scaffolding	direct modeling, manipulatives	primary	0122 at 203.jpg
123	0:36	Brooke, 1000 − 6	She takes 100 from 1000 and subtracts 6 from the 100 to get 94. Then because 1000 − 100 = 900, she answers 994.	F	5th	Caucasian	whole number subtraction, place value		composing/ decomposing numbers, invented strategy, number sense	intermediate	none
124	1:37	Brooke, 15 × 12	She knows 15 × 4 = 60. She adds up 3 sets of 60 to get 180. She relates it to the four 15-minute sections of the clock.	F	5th	Caucasian	whole number multiplication, story problem		invented strategy, composing/ decomposing numbers, number sense	intermediate, Exceptional Reasoning	none
125	2:25	Casey, 14 − 5	She directly models 14 − 5 with blocks. When asked to solve 14 − 6, she knows that it is 1 fewer than before.	F	1st	Latino	whole number subtraction, story problem	extension question	direct modeling, derived fact, manipulatives	primary	0125 at 151.jpg

CLIP #	TIME	TITLE	DESCRIPTION	GENDER	GRADE	ETHNICITY	CONTENT	TEACHING / INTERVIEWING	STRATEGY	MISC	SCREEN CAPTURE NAME
126	1:20	Cheyenne, 14 − 5	She directly models with blocks to solve.	F	1st	African American	whole number subtraction, story problem		direct modeling, manipulatives	primary	0126 at 105.jpg
127	1:34	Cheyenne, 18 ÷ 6	With blocks, she directly models 18 cupcakes shared by 3 children.	F	1st	African American	whole number division, story problem, equal sharing		manipulatives, direct modeling	primary	0127 at 102.jpg
128	1:22	Cheyenne, 4 + 7	She answers 12, but when asked to explain, realizes that she has made a mistake and says 11, because 7 + 3 = 10 and 1 more would be 11.	F	1st	African American	whole number addition, story problem		derived fact	self-corrects, primary, wrong answer	0128 at 050.jpg
129	1:20	Connor, 20 ÷ 4	With his fingers, he skip counts by fours to 20 and says 4. Measurement-division situation.	M	1st	Caucasian	whole number division, story problem	wait time	fingers, skip counting	wrong answer, primary	0129 at 113.jpg
130	0:44	Connor, 25 − 8	He knows that 8 is 5 plus 3 and uses this decomposition to solve the problem: 25 − 5 = 20, and 20 − 3 = 17.	M	1st	Caucasian	whole number subtraction, story problem		composing/decomposing numbers, invented strategy, number sense	primary, Exceptional Reasoning	none
131	2:59	Connor, 39 + 25	He says 61, because 20 + 39 = 59 and 2 more is 61. Reminded to add 25, he says 20 + 39 = 59 and 5 more is 64. Later (20 min.) to solve 39 + 25 without context, he adds (30 + 20) + (5 + 5) + 4.	M	1st	Caucasian	whole number addition, story problem, place value	clarify, probing, in/out of context	invented strategy, composing/decomposing numbers, number sense	primary, wrong answer	none
132	1:47	Connor, 4 × 25	He counts four 20s to 80. Then he adds the 5s and gets 20. Then he adds 80 + 20 and gets 100.	M	1st	Caucasian	whole number multiplication		skip counting, distributive property, repeated addition, number sense, composing/decomposing numbers, fingers	primary, Exceptional Reasoning	0132 at 122.jpg
133	1:03	Connor, 400 − 250	He solves 400 − 200 and gets 200, then solves 200 − 50.	M	1st	Caucasian	whole number subtraction, story problem, place value		composing/decomposing numbers, invented strategy, number sense	primary	none

CLIP #	TIME	TITLE	DESCRIPTION	GENDER	GRADE	ETHNICITY	CONTENT	TEACHING / INTERVIEWING	STRATEGY	MISC	SCREEN CAPTURE NAME
134	0:27	Connor, 6 + ? = 13	He knows that 6 + 6 = 12 and one more is 13.	M	1st	Caucasian	whole number addition, story problem, missing addend, whole number subtraction		derived fact	primary	none
135	1:04	Connor, 70 – 23	He knows that 70 – 20 = 50 and 50 – 3 = 47.	M	1st	Caucasian	whole number subtraction, place value		composing/ decomposing numbers, invented strategy, number sense	primary	none
136	0:34	Connor, 9 + 10 + 11	He says 30, because 9 + 10 = 19. 19 + 1 = 20 and 20 + 10 = 30.	M	1st	Caucasian	whole number addition		invented strategy, composing/ decomposing numbers, number sense	primary	none
137	1:36	Connor, 98 + 99	He initially answers 207. Then he changes his answer and explains that it is 17 + 180 and that 10 + 180 = 190 and 7 more is 197.	M	1st	Caucasian	whole number addition, place value		invented strategy, composing/ decomposing numbers, number sense	primary, self-corrects, wrong answer	none
138	2:02	Connor, baseball problem	He says 25 because he counted by threes 8 times (number of innings left) to 24 and added 1.	M	1st	Caucasian	whole number multiplication, story problem	wait time	skip counting, repeated addition, invented strategy	primary	none
139	1:24	Connor, cupcake problem	Initially answers using cupcakes as the unit then realizes that he needs to think of them as packages of 2. He says he counted by twos 6 times to 12 and then 12 – 2 = 10 and 10 – 3 = 7.	M	1st	Caucasian	story problem, whole number multiplication, whole number subtraction	clarify	skip counting, derived fact, composing/ decomposing numbers, invented strategy, repeated addition	primary, wrong answer, self-corrects	none
140	10:00	Dillon	He solves a series of problems that demonstrate the relative difficulties of the problems for a child.	M	2nd	Caucasian	whole number addition, missing addend, whole number subtraction, whole number multiplication, whole number division, equal sharing, story problem		counting on, fingers, standard algorithm, direct modeling, manipulatives, procedure	primary, wrong answer	140 at 941.jpg
141	1:08	Edgar, 14 – 5	He uses "fast nines" to solve. He explains that he has been taught that 14 – 4 = 10, and because 5 is 1 more than 4, the answer is 9.	M	1st	Latino	whole number subtraction, story problem		derived fact	primary	none

CLIP #	TIME	TITLE	DESCRIPTION	GENDER	GRADE	ETHNICITY	CONTENT	TEACHING / INTERVIEWING	STRATEGY	MISC	SCREEN CAPTURE NAME
142	0:32	Edgar, 4 × 25	He knows that 25 + 25 = 50 and that 50 + 50 = 100.	M	1st	Latino	whole number multiplication, story problem, money		derived fact, number sense	primary	none
143	2:02	Elizabeth, value of 200	Looking at a base-10 block representation of 200, she can see 200 candies, 20 rolls, and 2 hundreds.	F	3rd	Latino	place value	extension question, probing	number sense, manipulatives	primary	0143 at 048.jpg
144	2:29	Estephania, 1000 − 1	She solves 1000 − 1 using the standard algorithm. Interviewer asks her to think about doing it in her head. She is able to solve 1000 − 1 and 400 − 1 in her head. She says she likes doing it in her head better.	F	3rd	Latino	whole number subtraction, place value	extension question, probing	standard algorithm, procedure, number sense not evident	primary, Spanish speaker	0144 at 016.jpg
145	3:08	Estephania, rolls of candies	She knows that 4 rolls of 10 candies are 40. Ten rolls = 100 candies. She knows 20 rolls would be 200, because 20 is 2 times 10. She cannot see 20 rolls in the written numeral 200.	F	3rd	Latino	whole number multiplication, story problem, place value	extension question	recall, derived fact	primary, Spanish speaker, language issue	0145 at 152.jpg
146	4:56	Estephania, writing tens	PST asks her to write 10; she can. PST asks her to write 24 tens; she cannot. When asked to write 3 tens, she writes 10 three times. PST asks her to write 100 ones, she writes 101. When asked to write 10 hundred, she writes 110.	F	3rd	Latino	place value	difficult interview, scaffolding	misconception	primary, Spanish speaker, language issue	0146 at 438.jpg
147	1:30	Evelyn, 15 × 12	She visualizes the standard algorithm and explains with place-value understanding.	F	5th	Latino	whole number multiplication, story problem, place value		standard algorithm, procedure	intermediate, self-corrects, wrong answer	none
148	6:15	Freddie, 400 − 150, 150 + ? = 450	He gets three different answers when he solves these problems in four ways, but does not see the disconnect.	M	3rd	Latino	whole number subtraction, whole number addition, story problem, missing addend, place value	in/out of context, probing, extension question	standard algorithm, counting up, manipulatives, procedure, misconstrued strategy, number sense not evident, misconception	wrong answer, primary, cognitive dissonance	0148 at 536.jpg

CLIP #	TIME	TITLE	DESCRIPTION	GENDER	GRADE	ETHNICITY	CONTENT	TEACHING / INTERVIEWING	STRATEGY	MISC	SCREEN CAPTURE NAME
149	2:10	Freddie, 43 + ? = 100	He says that he used a "looping" method. He first adds 20 to 43 to get to 63, then adds 7 to 63 to get to 70, then adds 30 to 70 to get 100. He adds 20 + 7 + 30 = 57.	M	3rd	Latino	whole number addition, missing addend, story problem, whole number subtraction		procedure, counting up	primary, cognitive dissonance	0149 at 130.jpg
150	1:26	Gilberto, 12 × 15	He says that 12 × 10 is 120, and 5 × 12 is 60. Then he adds 120 + 60.	M	3rd	Latino	whole number multiplication, story problem, place value		distributive property, number sense	primary	none
151	0:36	Gilberto, 265 + 537	He adds 200 + 500 to get 700. Then adds 65 to 700 to get 765. He adds 30 to 765 to get 795. Then adds 7 to 795 and gets 802.	M	3rd	Latino	whole number addition, story problem, place value		composing/decomposing numbers, invented strategy, number sense	primary, Exceptional Reasoning	one
152	1:38	Gilberto, 451 – 169	He takes 100 from 451 and gets 351; 351 – 60 is 291, and 291 – 9 is 282.	M	3rd	Latino	whole number subtraction, story problem, place value	wait time	composing/decomposing numbers, number sense, invented strategy	primary, self-corrects, wrong answer	none
153	0:35	Gilberto, 65 + ? = 100	He knows that 60 + 40 = 100, then he subtracts 5 from 40 and gets 35.	M	3rd	Latino	whole number addition, story problem, missing addend, whole number subtraction		derived fact, composing/decomposing numbers	primary	none
154	0:41	Gino, 14 – 5	He knows that the answer is 9 because if it was 15 – 5 it would be 10, but it is 14 – 5, so he has 9.	M	1st	Caucasian	whole number subtraction, story problem		derived fact	primary	none
155	5:42	Gretchen, 70 – 23	She uses the standard algorithm incorrectly. When she uses the base-ten blocks and the hundred chart she gets the right answer. She thinks the first answer is correct.	F	1st	Caucasian	whole number subtraction, place value	probing	manipulatives, hundred chart, standard algorithm, procedure, misconstrued strategy	wrong answer, cognitive dissonance, primary	0155 at 514.jpg
156	2:27	Hally, 1000 – 6, 1000 – 1	She quickly solves the problems using the standard algorithm. She does not know how to solve it another way.	F	3rd	Asian American	whole number subtraction, place value	extension question	standard algorithm, procedure, number sense not evident	primary	0156 at 107.jpg

CLIP #	TIME	TITLE	DESCRIPTION	GENDER	GRADE	ETHNICITY	CONTENT	TEACHING / INTERVIEWING	STRATEGY	MISC	SCREEN CAPTURE NAME
157	0:36	Javier, 1000 – 6	He knows that 100 – 6 = 94, so 1000 – 6 = 994.	M	5th	Latino	whole number subtraction, place value		composing/decomposing numbers, number sense	intermediate, Spanish speaker	none
158	1:54	Javier, 6 × 12, then 12 × 12	He knows that 5 × 12 = 60 and 12 more is 72. He knew 5 × 12 = 60 because 10 × 12 = 120 and half of that is 60. He solves 12 × 12 because 12 × 10 = 120 and then 2 × 12 = 24 and 120 + 24 = 144.	M	5th	Latino	whole number multiplication, story problem, place value	extension question, probing	distributive property, number sense	intermediate, Spanish speaker	0158 at 043.jpg
159	0:24	Jennifer, 400 – 150	She says that 400 – 50 = 350 and that 350 – 100 more is 250.	F	3rd	Caucasian	whole number subtraction, story problem, place value		composing/decomposing numbers, number sense	primary	none
160	1:21	Jennifer, 7 × 12	She uses base-ten blocks to model 7 groups of 12. She makes a group of 10 using single blocks. She counts her groups of 10 and her single blocks and answers 84.	F	3rd	Caucasian	whole number multiplication, story problem, place value		direct modeling, manipulatives, number sense	primary	0160 at 053.jpg
161	1:58	Jessica, 100 – 3	She uses the standard algorithm to get 197. When asked how many pieces of gum she would have left if she had 100 and ate 3, she says 197. Interviewer reminds her that she started with 100. She says 97, but cannot explain.	F	3rd	Caucasian	whole number subtraction, story problem, place value	in/out of context, extension question	standard algorithm, procedure, number sense not evident	primary, wrong answer	0161 at 037.jpg
162	1:01	Jessica, 99 + 96	She visualizes the standard algorithm.	F	3rd	Caucasian	whole number addition		standard algorithm, procedure, number sense not evident	primary	none
163	4:03	Jessica, 38 + 45	PST models Julio's method (expanded algorithm) using base-ten blocks. Child uses the expanded algorithm and blocks to solve 38 + 45.	F	3rd	Caucasian	whole number addition, place value		expanded algorithm, direct modeling, manipulatives, procedure	primary	0163 at 226.jpg

CLIP #	TIME	TITLE	DESCRIPTION	GENDER	GRADE	ETHNICITY	CONTENT	TEACHING / INTERVIEWING	STRATEGY	MISC	SCREEN CAPTURE NAME
164	0:48	Jocelyn, 3 × 5	She counts by fives to find the number of sticks of gum in three 5-stick packs.	F	1st	Asian American	whole number multiplication, story problem		skip counting	primary	none
165	0:55	Jocelyn, 4 + 7	She counts on from 4 in her head to get 11.	F	1st	Asian American	whole number addition, story problem	wait time, probing	counting on	primary	none
166	0:53	Jocelyn, 6 + ? = 13	She knows that 6 + 6 = 12 and 7 + 7 = 14, so 6 + 7 = 13.	F	1st	Asian American	whole number addition, story problem, missing addend, whole number subtraction		derived fact	primary	0166 at 029.jpg
167	4:31	Johanna, 1000 − 4	She uses the standard algorithm (school way) and then counts back (thinking way). When asked whether the regrouped number is still 1000, she comes to see it as 900 + 90 + 10.	F	3rd	Caucasian	whole number subtraction, place value	probing	standard algorithm, counting back, procedure, number sense, composing/decomposing numbers	primary	0167 at 353.jpg
168	0:54	Johanna, 29 + 30 + 31	She uses a compensating strategy to correctly solve. She puts the 1 from 31 on 29 to make it 30; she adds the three 30s.	F	3rd	Caucasian	whole number addition		composing/decomposing numbers, number sense	primary	0168 at 034.jpg
169	1:03	Johanna, 12 × 12	She uses the standard algorithm to solve 6 × 12. To solve 12 × 12, she doubles her previous answer of 72.	F	3rd	Caucasian	whole number multiplication	probing	standard algorithm, derived fact, procedure, number sense	primary	0169 at 030.jpg
170	3:14	Kasage, 638 + 476	She has difficulty applying the expanded algorithm to a 3-digit addition problem. In her last attempt she adds 600 + 400 = 1000, 30 + 70 = 1000, and 8 + 6 = 14. Her total is 3014.	F	3rd	Caucasian	whole number addition, place value	scaffolding	expanded algorithm, procedure, number sense not evident	primary, wrong answer	0170 at 045.jpg
171	2:35	Michaela, 18 ÷ 3	She gives the wrong answer. Interviewer asks her to model the 18 with the blocks, and she continues to distribute the blocks into 3 groups.	F	1st	Caucasian	whole number division, story problem, equal sharing	scaffolding	direct modeling, manipulatives	primary, wrong answer	0171 at 221.jpg
172	0:25	Michaela, 5 + 3	She says that she just knows it.	F	1st	Caucasian	whole number addition, story problem		recall	primary	none
173	1:07	Michaela, 6 + ? = 13	She uses her fingers to count on from 6 to 13.	F	1st	Caucasian	whole number addition, missing addend, story problem	probing	fingers, counting on	primary	173 at 203 of 01mov.jpg

CLIP #	TIME	TITLE	DESCRIPTION	GENDER	GRADE	ETHNICITY	CONTENT	TEACHING / INTERVIEWING	STRATEGY	MISC	SCREEN CAPTURE NAME
174	0:24	Miguel, 10 + 11	He knows that 10 + 10 = 20, and 1 more is 21.	M	1st	Latino	whole number addition, story problem		derived fact	primary, Spanish speaker	none
175	0:33	Miguel, 25 × 4	He knows that 4 × 25 cents = $1.00 because he knows 4 quarters are in a dollar.	M	1st	Latino	money, story problem, whole number multiplication		recall, derived fact	primary, Spanish speaker	none
176	0:38	Miguel, 30 + 16	He knows that 30 + 10 = 40, and 40 + 6 = 46.	M	1st	Latino	whole number addition, story problem		composing/decomposing numbers	primary, Spanish speaker	none
177	0:46	Miguel, 6 + ? = 13	He knows that because 6 + 6 = 12, plus 7 is 13.	M	1st	Latino	whole number addition, story problem, missing addend, whole number subtraction		derived fact	primary, Spanish speaker	none
178	1:10	Mike, 100 – 1	He says 99. For 100 – 1 written horizontally, he writes 9. PST asks him to do 10 – 1. He writes 9.	M	3rd	Caucasian	whole number subtraction, place value	novice interviewer	standard algorithm, procedure, recall	primary, wrong answer, cognitive dissonance	0178 at 040.jpg
179	0:24	Mike, 5 + 3	He says that he has memorized that fact.	M	3rd	Caucasian	whole number addition, story problem		recall	primary	none
180	0:36	Mike, 70 – 23	He subtracts 20, then subtracts 3.	M	3rd	Caucasian	whole number subtraction, place value	novice interviewer	composing/decomposing numbers, number sense	primary	none
181	2:24	Myrna, 18 ÷ 3	She uses blocks to direct model dividing 18 M&Ms among 3 children. Translation provided.	F	2nd	Latino	whole number division, story problem, equal sharing		direct modeling, manipulatives	primary, Spanish speaker, language issue	0181 at 217.jpg
182	1:59	Myrna, 20 ÷ 4	She uses blocks to directly model; if there are 20 children and 4 ride in a car, how many cars are needed? She demonstrates good quantitative reasoning. Translation provided.	F	2nd	Latino	whole number division, story problem	clarify	direct modeling, manipulatives	primary, Spanish speaker, language issue	0182 at 130.jpg
183	0:59	Myrna, 3 × 5	She knows that 5 + 5 = 10, plus 5 more is 15. She has difficulty with the English word for fifteen.	F	2nd	Latino	whole number multiplication, story problem		repeated addition	primary, Spanish speaker, language issue	none
184	0:45	Myrna, 6 + ? = 13	She knows that 6 + 6 = 12 and adds one more to get 13.	F	2nd	Latino	whole number addition, story problem, missing addend, whole number subtraction		derived fact	primary, Spanish speaker, language issue	none

CLIP #	TIME	TITLE	DESCRIPTION	GENDER	GRADE	ETHNICITY	CONTENT	TEACHING / INTERVIEWING	STRATEGY	MISC	SCREEN CAPTURE NAME
185	1:00	Nicole, 18 ÷ 3	She directly models using blocks for 15 M&M's. She corrects when the interviewer clarifies that there are 18 M&M's.	F	2nd	Caucasian	whole number division, story problem, equal sharing	clarify	direct modeling, manipulatives	primary, wrong answer	185 at 057 in Select 23.jpg
186	1:15	Nicole, 20 ÷ 4	She guesses 8. Interviewer suggests she use blocks to show 20 children. She arranges 20 blocks in rows of 4. She counts the number of groups to tell the number of cars needed.	F	2nd	Caucasian	whole number division, story problem	scaffolding	manipulatives, direct modeling	primary, wrong answer	0186 at 110.jpg
187	0:56	Nicole, 6 + ? = 13	She pulls out 6 blocks, then adds more blocks to total 13. She counts the added blocks.	F	2nd	Caucasian	whole number subtraction, whole number addition, missing addend, story problem		direct modeling, manipulatives	primary	0187 at 049 in Select 1.jpg
188	0:15	Nicole, counts by tens	She counts by 10s to 100. She says that 200 comes after 100.	F	2nd	Caucasian	counting	extension question	skip counting, number sense not evident	primary, wrong answer	none
189	2:21	Nicole, 5 + 3, 7 + 4	She says 8, because she counted in her head. Interviewer asks if she used her fingers. She says that her teacher says not to use her fingers. For 7 + 4 she uses her fingers.	F	2nd	Caucasian	whole number addition, story problem	probing	counting on, fingers	primary	0189 at 218.jpg
190	1:17	Nicole, 14 − 5	She guesses 3. Interviewer suggests she use blocks. She directly models but miscounts and says 10.	F	2nd	Caucasian	whole number subtraction, story problem		manipulatives, direct modeling	primary, wrong answer	190 at 104 in Select 22.jpg
191	2:51	Petrisha, ? − 3 = 4	She answers incorrectly and says that she knows the answer "by thinking." PST asks her to solve the problem again, using blocks. The child eventually answers correctly and provides an explanation with blocks.	F	2nd	Latino	whole number subtraction, story problem	probing, novice interviewer, wait time	direct modeling, manipulatives	primary, wrong answer	0191 at 245.jpg
192	0:34	Petrisha, 5 + 3	She thinks 5 in her head and adds 3 more.	F	2nd	Latino	whole number addition, story problem		counting on	primary	none

117

CLIP #	TIME	TITLE	DESCRIPTION	GENDER	GRADE	ETHNICITY	CONTENT	TEACHING / INTERVIEWING	STRATEGY	MISC	SCREEN CAPTURE NAME
193	1:10	Petrisha, 6 + ? = 13, part unknown, 8, 5	For the first problem she answers 7 and counts from 1 to 7 on her fingers to explain. Interviewer accepts this explanation, adding her own interpretation. Interviewer probes more deeply the child's explanation for the second problem.	F	2nd	Latino	whole number addition, whole number subtraction, missing addend, story problem	probing, difficult interview, novice interviewer	counting on, fingers	primary	0193 at 108.jpg
194	0:45	Petrisha, part unknown, 8, 14	She says that she thought of the blue marbles and then counted the rest (6 red marbles) on her fingers.	F	2nd	Latino	story problem, whole number addition, whole number subtraction, missing addend		counting on, fingers	primary	0194 at 019.jpg
195	1:42	Rachel, 45 × 36	She rewrites the problem horizontally. She multiplies 40 × 30, then 40 × 6, 5 × 30, and 5 × 6. She then adds the four products.	F	5th	Caucasian	whole number multiplication, place value, algebra		distributive property, expanded algorithm, procedure	intermediate, Exceptional Reasoning	0195 at 138.jpg
196	1:03	Rosa, 10 × 4	She adds 10 + 10 = 20 and then 20 + 20 = 40.	F	1st	Latino	money, whole number multiplication, story problem		repeated addition	Spanish speaker, primary, language issue	0196 at 031.jpg
197	2:23	Rosa, 20 ÷ 4	She thinks that the problem is 13 ÷ 4 and draws an appropriate solution. Interviewer clarifies the problem in Spanish. She then continues to draw the solution for 20 ÷ 4.	F	1st	Latino	whole number division, story problem	clarify	drawing	language issue, primary, Spanish speaker	0197 at 209.jpg
198	1:56	Shannon, 20 × ? = 140	She counts by 20s to get to 100, and knows that she counted five 20s. Then she knows that 40 is two more 20s. She knows that 5 + 2 = 7.	F	3rd	Caucasian	whole number multiplication, story problem, whole number division, place value		skip counting, fingers, invented strategy, number sense, composing/ decomposing numbers	primary, Exceptional Reasoning	0198 at 152.jpg
199	0:43	Shannon, 4 × 15	She knows that each 15 is three 5s. She counts by 5s.	F	3rd	Caucasian	whole number multiplication, story problem		skip counting, fingers, composing/ decomposing numbers, number sense	primary	0199 at 033.jpg

CLIP #	TIME	TITLE	DESCRIPTION	GENDER	GRADE	ETHNICITY	CONTENT	TEACHING / INTERVIEWING	STRATEGY	MISC	SCREEN CAPTURE NAME
200	2:09	Talecia, 34 + 57	She uses the standard algorithm to solve. Interviewer asks her to explain the 1 she "carried" when adding 4 + 7. She does not seem to discriminate between that 1 (ten) and the 1 in the one's place in 11.	F	3rd	African American	whole number addition, place value	extension question	standard algorithm, manipulatives, procedure	primary	0200 at 159.jpg
201	7:21	Talecia, 638 + 476	She uses the expanded algorithm to solve, but writes 110 for 10 hundred when she adds 400 + 600. PST attempts to scaffold her understanding.	F	3rd	African American	whole number addition, place value	scaffolding, novice interviewer	expanded algorithm, manipulatives, procedure, misconception	primary, cognitive dissonance, wrong answer	0201 at 152.jpg
202	1:15	Taylor, 9 + 4	She says that 9 + 4 = 13. She started with 9 and counted 4 fingers up to 13.	F	3rd	Caucasian	whole number addition, story problem	probing, difficult interview	counting on, fingers	primary	none
203	1:57	Taylor, comparison 4, 9	She writes 9 and 4 on her paper but seems puzzled. She knows who has more. Interviewer asks her to compare 8 and 9; she uses that prompt to answer the original question correctly.	F	3rd	Caucasian	story problem, comparison, whole number addition, whole number subtraction	scaffolding, wait time, novice interviewer	counting on, fingers	primary	0204 at 214.jpg
204	2:35	Taylor, Racing to a Flat	PST and child play a place-value game called "Racing to a Flat."	F	3rd	Caucasian	place value	difficult interview	manipulatives, direct modeling	primary	0204 at 214.jpg
205	2:02	Tracy, 14 − 5	She uses her fingers and answers zero. Interviewer asks what 5 − 5 equals? She realizes that the differences cannot both equal zero. She then directly models with blocks to solve correctly.	F	1st	Caucasian	whole number subtraction, story problem		direct modeling, fingers, manipulatives	primary, cognitive dissonance, wrong answer	0205 at 148.jpg
206	2:19	Vanessa, 1000 − 4	She solves it using the standard algorithm.	F	4th	Latino	whole number subtraction, place value	probing	standard algorithm, procedure, number sense not evident	intermediate	0206 at 041.jpg

CLIP #	TIME	TITLE	DESCRIPTION	GENDER	GRADE	ETHNICITY	CONTENT	TEACHING / INTERVIEWING	STRATEGY	MISC	SCREEN CAPTURE NAME
207	1:23	Zenaida, value of 32, 120, 316	She knows that there are 3 tens in 32 because 3 × 10 = 30. There are 12 tens in 120 because 10 × 10 = 100, plus 2 more tens = 120. There are 316 ones in 316 and 32 ones in 32.	F	3rd	Latino	place value		distributive property, composing/decomposing numbers, number sense	primary, Exceptional Reasoning	0207 at 106.jpg
300	0:50	Ally, 1/7	When asked to consider 7/6, she sees the extra sixth as 1/7.	F	5th	Caucasian	fractions, role of the unit, identifying fractions		direct modeling, manipulatives, misconception	intermediate, wrong answer	0300 at 048.jpg
301	0:56	Ally, 3 – 5/6	She draws to find the answer.	F	3rd	Caucasian	fraction subtraction, story problem, fractions		drawing, direct modeling	primary	0301 at 033.jpg
302	4:31	Ally, compare & convert fractions	She compares and converts fractions and explains her thinking.	F	5th	Caucasian	fractions, comparison, renaming fractions	probing, extension question	misconstrued strategy, misconception	wrong answer, intermediate	0302at 259.jpg
303	3:54	Ally, converting fractions	Interviewer shows Ally how to convert mixed numbers to improper fractions, using only a procedure.	F	5th	Caucasian	fractions, renaming fractions	procedural instruction	procedure, standard algorithm	intermediate	0303 at 302.jpg
304	6:34	Ally, fractions with pattern blocks	Interviewer helps Ally explore fraction concepts with pattern blocks.	F	5th	Caucasian	fractions, identifying fractions	scaffolding, conceptual instruction	direct modeling, manipulatives	intermediate	0304 at 634.jpg
305	2:53	Andrew, decimal assessment	He correctly adds but incorrectly compares decimals. He consistently chooses the larger numeral, disregarding the decimal point.	M	3rd	Caucasian	comparison, decimal addition, decimals		misconception	primary	305 at 413 in Select 08 jpg
306	0:35	Brooke, 3 – 5/6	She knows that she can put aside 2 if only part of 1 cookie is eaten, so she still has two. Because one whole is 6/6, taking away 5/6 leaves one part, so 2 and 1/6.	F	5th	Caucasian	fraction subtraction, story problem, fractions		number sense	intermediate	none
307	1:26	Brooke, 4 – .7	She draws 4 circles and divides the first circle into tenths. She writes 10 in each of the other 3 circles. She shades .7 of the first circle. She says that .3 of the circle is left, writes $3\frac{3}{10}$ and then 3.3.	F	5th	Caucasian	decimal subtraction, decimals, fractions		drawing, direct modeling	ntermediate	307 at 113 in Select 10.jpg

CLIP #	TIME	TITLE	DESCRIPTION	GENDER	GRADE	ETHNICITY	CONTENT	TEACHING / INTERVIEWING	STRATEGY	MISC	SCREEN CAPTURE NAME
308	1:14	Daisy, cf 1/2 and 1/3, 1 and 5/4	She compares 1/2 and 1/3, saying that the 1/2 is halves and they are bigger than three little pieces. She says that 1 is larger than 5/4, but when asked if 5/4 is more or less than one pie, she says that it is more than one pie.	F	2nd	Latino	fractions, comparison	probing	number sense, misconception	primary, wrong answer, technology	0308 at 014.jpg
309	2:41	Daisy, cf 1/3 and 1/4	Guided by the interviewer, she uses a computer application to help her think about the sizes of fractional pieces.	F	2nd	Latino	fractions, comparison	scaffolding	drawing	primary, technology	0309 at 203.jpg
310	0:18	Daisy, names 1/4 as 1/3	In a circle partitioned to show 1 half and 2 fourths she names 1/4 as 1/3 because there are three pieces, and if you eat one piece, it is 1/3.	F	2nd	Latino	fractions, identifying fractions		misconception	primary, wrong answer, technology	0310 at 008.jpg
311	0:49	David, converts $2\frac{1}{4}$ (post concept)	He converts $2\frac{1}{4}$ to 9/4 using the standard algorithm. He explains nicely that there are 8 fourths in 2 and one more fourth is 9 fourths. (unclear sound)	M	5th	Caucasian	fractions, renaming fractions		procedure, standard algorithm	intermediate	0311 at 029.jpg
312	2:26	David, converts $2\frac{1}{4}$ (post proced)	He "timesed" the 4 by the 1 and got 5. He then moved the 2 (whole number) to the denominator.	M	5th	Caucasian	fractions, renaming fractions	probing, wait time	misconstrued strategy	intermediate, wrong answer	0312 at 137.jpg
313	1:39	David, # of 5ths in 3 wholes	He says 15. He multiplies 3 × 5 because each whole is 5 fifths and there are 3 wholes.	M	5th	Caucasian	fractions, renaming fractions		number sense	intermediate	0313 at 056.jpg
314	1:15	Eduardo, 1/3 class is boys	PST asks whether the class has more boys or girls if 1/3 of the class is boys. Child says that they are half and half. He puts 3 pattern blocks together to make a whole and then says that one third and another third make half of a whole.	M	5th	Latino	fractions, story problem	probing	direct modeling, manipulatives	wrong answer, intermediate	0314 at 056.jpg

121

CLIP #	TIME	TITLE	DESCRIPTION	GENDER	GRADE	ETHNICITY	CONTENT	TEACHING / INTERVIEWING	STRATEGY	MISC	SCREEN CAPTURE NAME
315	1:57	Eduardo, 1/4 of 1/2	When shown a circle partitioned into 1/2 and 4/8, he says that one of the eighths is 1/6? 1/4? Interviewer asks 1/4 of what? He says that it is 1/4 of 1/2.	M	5th	Latino	fractions, identifying fractions	probing, scaffolding	misconception	wrong answer, intermediate	0315 at 046.jpg
316	3:02	Eduardo, 4 shared by 3	He says that each gets 1 whole and 1/6. PST asks him to draw the cookies. He divides the fourth cookie into 6 pieces and says that each gets a whole and a triangle. He does not know why he cut the cookie into 6 pieces.	M	5th	Latino	fractions, equal sharing, story problem, whole number division, identifying fractions	probing	drawing, direct modeling	wrong answer, intermediate	0316 at 224.jpg
317	2:09	Eduardo, 6 – 1/4	He says $5\frac{3}{4}$, because 4/4 is one whole and if you take away 1 (fourth), you have 3/4 left.	M	5th	Latino	fraction subtraction, story problem, fractions	wait time	number sense	intermediate	0317 at 207.jpg
318	2:00	Eduardo, 7 shared by 4	PST draws 7 cookies and explains that all the cookies and each person wants some of each cookie. He partitions each cookie into fourths and says each person gets 1/4 of 7 cookies. PST asks how much cookie that is in all.	M	5th	Latino	fractions, equal sharing, story problem, whole number division	probing	drawing, direct modeling	intermediate	0318 at 058.jpg
319	0:34	Eduardo, naming fraction (1/4)	Interviewer shows him a circle divided into fourths and asks what each piece is called. He says a third? Interviewer asks why a third?	M	5th	Latino	fractions, identifying fractions	extension question	misconception	wrong answer, intermediate	
320	2:28	Elaine, 3 shared by 2, 1 shared by 4	She is shown 3 circles. She says that each would get 1, and cut the last one in half. She names it $1\frac{1}{2}$. When shown 1 cookie shared by 4 people, she divides it into fourths and says each gets a quarter. She draws a coin (quarter).	F	1st	Caucasian	fractions, equal sharing, story problem, whole number division		drawing, direct modeling	primary	0320 at 221.jpg

CLIP #	TIME	TITLE	DESCRIPTION	GENDER	GRADE	ETHNICITY	CONTENT	TEACHING / INTERVIEWING	STRATEGY	MISC	SCREEN CAPTURE NAME
321	1:29	Elliot, $1 \div 1/3$, then $1\frac{1}{2} \div 1/3$	He is able to solve $1 \div 1/3$ by using his understanding of division. When given a similar problem, he uses the same reasoning but loses sight of the unit.	M	6th	Caucasian	fraction division, role of the unit, fractions		drawing, number sense, misconception	intermediate, wrong answer	0321 at 031.jpg
322	1:07	Evelyn, $4 - .7$	She says 3.3, because 10 parts equal a whole and if you took away 7, that equals 3. So if it was 4 and you took a whole away, that equals 3.	F	5th	Latino	decimal subtraction, decimals		invented strategy, number sense	intermediate	none
323	0:56	Everett, converts $3\frac{1}{8}$ (post concept)	He converts $3\frac{1}{8}$ correctly. He elegantly explains how it works.	M	5th	Caucasian	fractions, renaming fractions		number sense	intermediate, Exceptional Reasoning	0323 at 055.jpg
324	1:29	Everett, converts $3\frac{1}{8}$ (post proced)	He converts $3\frac{1}{8}$ to 3/8.	M	5th	Caucasian	fractions, renaming fractions	probing	misconstrued strategy	intermediate, wrong answer	0324 at 027.jpg
325	3:10	Felisha, 1 shared by 4, then by 3	She draws the problem and sees that each gets 1/4. Interviewer asks what each gets if one child leaves. She draws in the twelfths and says that they get 1/4 and 1/12. She knows that 1/4 + 1/12 = 1/3.	F	4th	African American	fractions, equal sharing, story problem, role of the unit, identifying fractions, whole number division	probing	direct modeling, drawing, number sense	intermediate, Exceptional Reasoning	Clip 325 work.pdf
326	2:29	Felisha, 2 shared by 5	If 5 people share 2 cookies, how much does each person get? She says that each get 1/5 of each cookie or 2/10 of both cookies.	F	4th	African American	fractions, equal sharing, role of the unit, whole number division	probing	drawing, direct modeling	intermediate	326 at 101 in Select 14.jpg
327	1:37	Felisha, 2/3 of 12	She answers 8, because 12 divided by 3 is 4, and 4 more is 8, and that's 2/3. She reasons similarly to solve 3/4 of 12.	F	4th	African American	fraction multiplication, story problem, fractions		number sense	intermediate	none
328	1:41	Felisha, 2/8 = 1/4	She knows that a rectangle divided into eighths, with the 1st and 5th sections shaded, shows 2/8. She can also see and explain why it shows 1/4.	F	2nd	African American	fractions, renaming fractions, identifying fractions		number sense	primary	0328 at 131.jpg

CLIP #	TIME	TITLE	DESCRIPTION	GENDER	GRADE	ETHNICITY	CONTENT	TEACHING / INTERVIEWING	STRATEGY	MISC	SCREEN CAPTURE NAME
329	1:39	Felisha, 3/4 + 1/2	She solves problem correctly. She uses drawings of circles to support her reasoning. She has not been taught to add fractions.	F	2nd	African American	fraction addition, fractions		drawing, direct modeling	primary, Exceptional Reasoning	0329 at 133.jpg
330	4:54	Felisha, 3/4 of 2	She partitions 1 of 2 circles into 4ths, shades 3 of 4 parts, and writes $1\frac{1}{4}$ left. Interviewer clarifies that she means 3/4 of the package of cupcakes. Child draws 2 more circles, partitions them in halves, writes 1/2, and answers 3/2 cupcakes.	F	2nd	African American	fraction multiplication, story problem, role of the unit, fractions	clarify	drawing, direct modeling	primary, Exceptional Reasoning	0330 at 411.jpg
331	2:47	Felisha, $4\frac{1}{8}$ − 7/8	She solves problem correctly. She uses drawings of circles to support her reasoning. She has not been taught fraction subtraction.	F	2nd	African American	fractions, fraction subtraction		drawing, direct modeling	primary, wrong answer, self-corrects	0331 at 158.jpg
332	2:40	Felisha, $5\frac{3}{4}$ divided by 1/2	In $5\frac{3}{4}$ pounds of jelly beans, how many 1/2-pound bags? After she says 6, the interviewer reminds her that they are 1/2-pound bags; she says 12. She explains her reasoning, and tells how much of the last bag is filled.	F	4th	African American	fraction division, story problem, fractions	clarify	number sense	intermediate, wrong answer	0332 at 223.jpg
333	0:50	Felisha, 5 shared by 4	She shares her solution. The interviewer helps her count 1/4, 2/4, 3/4, 4/4, 5/4. Video clip includes a still picture of her work.	F	2nd	African American	fractions, equal sharing, story problem, whole number division	small group, student discourse, scaffolding	drawing, direct modeling	primary	
334	2:09	Felisha, 6 − 1/4 of each	She draws six circles and partitions each circle into fourths. She shades 1/4 of each circle and counts the unshaded fourths. She writes 18/4 and then tells how she knows that it is $4\frac{1}{2}$.	F	2nd	African American	fraction subtraction, story problem, renaming fractions, fractions		drawing, direct modeling	primary	0334 at 121.jpg

CLIP #	TIME	TITLE	DESCRIPTION	GENDER	GRADE	ETHNICITY	CONTENT	TEACHING / INTERVIEWING	STRATEGY	MISC	SCREEN CAPTURE NAME
335	1:34	Felisha, 6 – 1/4 (post)	She draws six circles and partitions one circle into fourths. She writes $5\frac{3}{4}$ and explains her answer.	F	2nd	African American	fraction subtraction, story problem, fractions		drawing, direct modeling	primary	0335 at 117.jpg
336	2:02	Felisha, 6 – 1/4 (pre)	She draws 6 circles. She draws another circle and divides it into fourths. She thinks that the answer is $5\frac{1}{3}$.	F	2nd	African American	fraction subtraction, story problem, identifying fractions, fractions	wait time	drawing, direct modeling, misconception	primary, wrong answer	0336 at 116.jpg
337	1:48	Felisha, estimate 9/10 + 6/7	She is asked to estimate the sum. She draws both fractions and says that she thinks that the sum is close to 2.	F	4th	African American	fraction addition, fractions		direct modeling, drawing, number sense	intermediate	0337 at 128.jpg
338	1:22	Felisha, compares fractions	She incorrectly compares 2/4 and 1/2, 4/3 and 1, 3/6 and 5/8 by adding the numerals within the fractions and comparing the sums.	F	2nd	African American	fractions, comparison		misconstrued strategy, misconception	primary, wrong answer	0338 at 039.jpg
339	1:48	Felisha, draw $1\frac{3}{4}$	She draws a circle. Then she draws three rectangles each partitioned into fourths.	F	2nd	African American	fractions, identifying fractions		drawing	primary, wrong answer	0339 at 111.jpg
340	3:06	Felisha, identifying fractions	She is shown a rectangle partitioned into fifths. She names the different fractions when the interviewer changes the unit.	F	4th	African American	fractions, identifying fractions, role of the unit	extension question	number sense	intermediate	0340 at 247.jpg
341	3:51	Francisco, 4 – 1/8	He does not know how to solve the problem using only the numbers. When given the problem in context, he draws 4 circles and partitions one circle into eighths. He shades 1/8 and says $3\frac{7}{8}$.	M	5th	Latino	fraction subtraction, story problem, fractions	in/out of context, extension question	drawing, direct modeling	intermediate	0341 at 346.jpg
342	1:26	Jace, 1/5 cf 1/8	When he compares 1/5 and 1/8 in the context of chocolate bars, he says 1/5 is larger. Out of context, he circles 1/8 as the larger fraction.	M	4th	Caucasian	comparison, fractions	in/out of context	misconception, number sense not evident	intermediate, wrong answer, cognitive dissonance	0342 at 114.pct

125

CLIP #	TIME	TITLE	DESCRIPTION	GENDER	GRADE	ETHNICITY	CONTENT	TEACHING / INTERVIEWING	STRATEGY	MISC	SCREEN CAPTURE NAME
343	0:50	Jacky, compare fractions	She thinks that 1 = 4/4, but 1 > 4/3.	F	5th	Caucasian	comparison, fractions		misconception, number sense not evident	intermediate, wrong answer	none
344	1:33	Jacky, 1/2 + 1/4	She adds the numerators and then divides the denominator (4) by 2. She says that the answer is 2/2 or 1.	F	5th	Caucasian	fraction addition, fractions		misconstrued strategy, number sense not evident	intermediate, wrong answer	0344 at 056.jpg
345	10:19	Jacky, 2/7 cf 1/7	Using "out of" language, she thinks that 1/7 > 2/7 because what is "left over" is larger. The interviewer helps her clarify her thinking. A PST shares a similar experience.	F	5th	Caucasian	comparison, fractions	scaffolding, novice interviewer	misconception, drawing	intermediate, wrong answer, teacher reflection/ advice	0345 at 519.jpg
346	4:28	Jacky, 4 – 1/8	She rewrites the problem vertically and answers "4-1/8," because 1/8 take away zero is still 1/8. In context, she answers 3 wholes and 1/7, because there are 7 pieces left.	F	5th	Caucasian	fraction subtraction, story problem, fractions, role of the unit	in/out of context, probing, novice interviewer	misconception, misconstrued strategy, drawing	intermediate, wrong answer	0346 at 218.jpg
347	0:54	Jacky, 4 shared by 3	She draws 4 brownies and partitions 1 into thirds.	F	5th	Caucasian	equal sharing, story problem, whole number division, fractions		drawing, direct modeling	intermediate	0347 at 046.jpg
348	1:15	Jacky, partitions a whole	Although interviewer raises the issue of equal-sized pieces in a representation of 1/6, when the child shows thirds as 1 half and 2 fourths, interviewer does not comment on the representation.	F	5th	Caucasian	fractions, comparison, identifying fractions, story problem	novice interviewer	misconception, drawing	intermediate	0348 at 111.jpg
349	0:56	Javier, 3 – 5/6	He knows that 5/6 from 1 is 1/6. There are two (wholes) left over, so the answer is $2\frac{1}{6}$.	M	5th	Latino	fraction subtraction, story problem, fractions		number sense	intermediate, Spanish speaker	
350	0:40	Javier, 4 – .7	He answers 3 and 3 tenths. He changes the .7 into 7/10 and knows there will be 3/10 left. He adds the three wholes for $3\frac{3}{10}$.	M	5th	Latino	decimal subtraction, decimals		number sense	intermediate	0350 at 034.jpg

CLIP #	TIME	TITLE	DESCRIPTION	GENDER	GRADE	ETHNICITY	CONTENT	TEACHING / INTERVIEWING	STRATEGY	MISC	SCREEN CAPTURE NAME
351	2:05	Javier, 9 ÷ 3/4	He uses 45/60 to represent the 3/4. He knows to add 15/60 to get one whole. So to make 9 wholes you would need 9 (15/60) pieces. Nine of these (15/60) would make 3 of the 45/60 pieces, which added to the 9 (for which the unit is 45/60) makes 12.	M	5th	Latino	fraction division, story problem, role of the unit, fractions		invented strategy	intermediate, Exceptional Reasoning	none
352	1:03	Johanna, 1/2 + 1/4	She knows that 1/2 = 2/4 because the top numbers are half of the bottom numbers.	F	3rd	Caucasian	fraction addition, story problem, fractions		invented strategy	primary	0352 at 102.jpg
353	1:20	Johanna, 6 – 1/4	She solves it mentally and draws a picture to explain.	F	3rd	Caucasian	fraction subtraction, story problem, fractions		number sense, drawing	primary	0353 at 107.jpg
354	0:56	Johanna, 7/3 = 2⅓	She is able to articulate why they are the same.	F	3rd	Caucasian	fractions, renaming fractions		number sense	primary	none
355	6:42	Josh, 3/4 × 1/2 and 1/4 × 4/5	With the interviewer's guidance, he uses a computer application to help him think about multiplication of fractions.	M	5th	Caucasian	fraction multiplication, role of the unit, fractions	scaffolding	drawing	intermediate, wrong answer, technology	0355 of 352. jpg
356	0:25	Madison, 1/2 + 1/3	She thinks that the answer is 2/5 because 1 + 1 = 2 and 2 + 3 = 5.	F	5th	Caucasian	fraction addition, fractions		misconstrued strategy, misconception	intermediate, wrong answer	none
357	1:54	Madison, 3/4 on number line	She places 3/4 between the 3 and the 4 on the number line. PST asks her if 1 > 3/4?	F	5th	Caucasian	fractions	scaffolding	misconception, number sense not evident	intermediate, wrong answer	0357 at 013.jpg
358	2:34	Madison, decimal assessment	She compares decimal numbers by choosing the larger number without regard to location of the decimal point. She adds decimal numbers correctly.	F	5th	Caucasian	decimal addition, comparison, decimals		standard algorithm, procedure, misconstrued strategy, misconception	intermediate, wrong answer	0358 at 221.jpg
359	0:19	Madison, estimate 9/10 + 6/7	She chooses 15 from the choices given and explains that she added the numerators.	F	5th	Caucasian	fractions, fraction addition		misconception, number sense not evident	intermediate, wrong answer	None

CLIP #	TIME	TITLE	DESCRIPTION	GENDER	GRADE	ETHNICITY	CONTENT	TEACHING / INTERVIEWING	STRATEGY	MISC	SCREEN CAPTURE NAME
360	1:56	Markie, cf $2\frac{3}{8}$ and 19/8 (post proced)	Using a procedure, she says that $2\frac{3}{8} = 19/8$. She cannot explain why they are equal.	F	5th	Caucasian	fractions, comparison, renaming fractions	probing, wait time	procedure, standard algorithm, number sense not evident	intermediate	none
361	2:26	Markie, converts $3\frac{3}{8}$ (post concept)	She converts $3\frac{3}{8}$ to an improper fraction using the procedure and is able to explain how it works.	F	5th	Caucasian	fractions, renaming fractions	probing, wait time	standard algorithm, procedure, number sense	intermediate	0361 at 024.jpg
362	2:28	Markie, converts 9/5	She correctly converts 9/5 to $1\frac{4}{5}$ using the standard algorithm, but she does not know why one divides the 5 into the 9.	F	5th	Caucasian	fractions, renaming fractions		standard algorithm, procedure, number sense not evident	intermediate	none
363	0:54	Melissa, compares 5/3 and $1\frac{2}{3}$	She thinks that 5/3 and $1\frac{2}{3}$ are equal because 5×3 (from 5/3) is 15, and if you add the 2 and the 3 (in 2/3) and put it next to the one ($1\frac{2}{3}$), it is also 15.	F	5th	Caucasian	fractions, comparison, renaming fractions	probing	misconstrued strategy	intermediate	363 at 027 in Select 25.jpg
364	3:12	Myrna, 8 shared by 6	She uses blocks to model and knows that each of the two wholes left over needs to be divided into three pieces. She partitions both drawn brownies into thirds. Translation provided.	F	2nd	Latino	fractions, equal sharing, story problem, whole number division		direct modeling, drawing, manipulatives	primary, Spanish speaker, language issue	0364 at 309.jpg
365	5:45	Nico, 1/2 + 1/3, 5/6 − 1/2	He works both, writing them vertically and changing to common denominators. Interviewer has him use pattern blocks to build wholes; he writes equations for the combinations he creates. He is asked, "Which is more, 2/6 or 1/3?"	M	5th	Caucasian	fraction addition, fraction subtraction, fractions	scaffolding	procedure, direct modeling, manipulatives, standard algorithm	intermediate	0365 at 129.jpg; 0365 at 434.jpg
366	3:59	Rachel, converts $3\frac{3}{8}$ (post concept)	She converts $3\frac{3}{8}$ using the procedure incorrectly. When she draws a solution, she sees that it does not match her answer. When she describes the drawing, she self-corrects. She articulates how the procedure interferes with her understanding.	F	5th	Caucasian	fractions, renaming fractions	scaffolding	procedure, drawing, misconstrued strategy, direct modeling	intermediate, wrong answer, self-corrects, cognitive dissonance, Exceptional Reasoning	0366 at 131.jpg

CLIP #	TIME	TITLE	DESCRIPTION	GENDER	GRADE	ETHNICITY	CONTENT	TEACHING / INTERVIEWING	STRATEGY	MISC	SCREEN CAPTURE NAME
367	1:20	Rachel, converts $3\frac{3}{8}$ (post proced)	She tries to convert $3\frac{3}{8}$. She cannot remember because she did not get to figure out the procedure for herself.	F	5th	Caucasian	fractions, renaming fractions	probing		intermediate, Exceptional Reasoning	0367 at 040.jpg
368	0:53	Rachel, converts 9/5	She divides 9 into 5 and thinks that the answer is $5\frac{5}{9}$. When asked why she divided the 9 into the 5, she says that is what she was taught.	F	5th	Caucasian	fractions, renaming fractions	probing	misconstrued strategy, number sense not evident	intermediate, wrong answer	0368 at 036.jpg
369	1:24	Sean, 1 – 1/7	Initially he answers 1/6 until the PST asks him to write the 1 as a fraction. He writes 7/7 and then answers 6/7.	M	5th	Caucasian	fraction subtraction, fractions	novice interviewer, scaffolding	misconstrued strategy	intermediate, wrong answer, self-corrects	0369 at 101.jpg
370	1:35	Sean, 1/2 + 1/3	He thinks that he can use the lowest common denominator to change each fraction to 1/6. He adds the numerators to get 2/6.	M	5th	Caucasian	fraction addition, renaming fractions, fractions		standard algorithm, procedure, misconstrued strategy, number sense not evident	intermediate, wrong answer	0370 at 108.jpg
371	1:35	Sean, 3/4 on the # line	He places 3/4 between the 3 and the 4 on the number line.	M	5th	Caucasian	fractions, identifying fractions		number sense not evident, misconception	intermediate, wrong answer	0371 at 032.jpg
372	0:29	Sean, 3/6 – 1/2	He knows that 1/2 = 3/6, because 1 + 1 = 2 and 3 + 3 = 6. So the answer is 0.	M	5th	Caucasian	fraction subtraction, fractions		number sense	intermediate	none
373	1:45	Sean, compares fractions	He compares several fractions successfully (1/6 and 1/8, 2/7 and 1/7, 1 and 4/4, 1/2 and 3/6, 1 and 4/3).	M	5th	Caucasian	fractions, comparison			intermediate	0373 at 145.pct
374	1:32	Sean, converts $4\frac{1}{3}$ and 13/6	He converts $4\frac{1}{3}$ to 5/3 because you add the 4 "into" the 1/3. He converts 13/6 to $8\frac{5}{6}$ with a convoluted strategy.	M	5th	Caucasian	fractions, renaming fractions		misconstrued strategy, number sense not evident	intermediate, wrong answer	0374 at 115.pct
375	2:31	Sean, decimal assessment	To compare decimals, he chooses one-digit numbers as the larger because they are closer to 1 or to 0. He adds decimal numbers correctly.	M	5th	Caucasian	decimal addition, comparison, decimals		standard algorithm, procedure, misconstrued strategy, misconception	intermediate, wrong answer	0375 at 224.jpg

CLIP #	TIME	TITLE	DESCRIPTION	GENDER	GRADE	ETHNICITY	CONTENT	TEACHING / INTERVIEWING	STRATEGY	MISC	SCREEN CAPTURE NAME
376	1:46	Sean, estimate 9/10 + 6/7	He uses the lowest common-denominator reasoning to choose "None" as his answer. Neither 10 nor 7 will "meet up" with any of the multiple-choice answers.	M	5th	Caucasian	fraction addition, fractions		standard algorithm, procedure, number sense not evident	intermediate, wrong answer	0376 at 130.jpg
377	0:41	Shelby, 12 ÷ 1/2	She answers 24 because if it takes half a foot of ribbon for each box, you just double it. So you have 2 boxes for every foot, therefore 24 boxes.	F	5th	Caucasian	fraction division, story problem, fractions		number sense	intermediate	
378	1:12	Shelby, 4 – .7	She draws four circles and partitions the first one into tenths. She says that she needs only one because the other three are left over. She knows that 7 + 3 = 10, so she uses 7 of that (first circle), and three whole ones are left.	F	5th	Caucasian	decimal subtraction, decimals		drawing, direct modeling, number sense	intermediate	0378 at 037.jpg
379	4:53	Stephanie, adding fractions	A PST helps a student think about fractional pieces when adding three sixths and one half using pattern blocks. However, when asked to represent the sum with a written expression, she writes 1/2 + 3/6 = 4/8.	F	5th	Caucasian	fraction addition, identifying fractions, fractions	difficult interview, extension question, probing, scaffolding	procedure, manipulatives, misconstrued strategy, misconception	intermediate, wrong answer, cognitive dissonance	0379 at 451.jpg
380	5:18	Trina, division of fractions	She is taught how to divide fractions using the standard algorithm, but 3 days later she cannot apply the algorithm correctly.	F	4th	Latino	fractions, fraction division	procedural instruction, wait time	standard algorithm, procedure, misconstrued strategy	intermediate, wrong answer	0380 at 425.jpg
381	0:49	Vanessa, 1/6 missing	Looking at a model of 5/6, she thinks that it is called 1/5, because 1/6 is missing.	F	5th	Latino	identifying fractions, fractions	probing	misconception	intermediate, wrong answer	0381 at 020.jpg
382	4:56	Vanessa, 10/3	After some scaffolding, she explains the number of wholes and thirds in 10/3. She counts by threes because one whole is 3 thirds.	F	5th	Latino	fractions, renaming fractions	conceptual instruction, scaffolding, novice interviewer, extension question	number sense	intermediate	0382 at 347.pct

CLIP #	TIME	TITLE	DESCRIPTION	GENDER	GRADE	ETHNICITY	CONTENT	TEACHING / INTERVIEWING	STRATEGY	MISC	SCREEN CAPTURE NAME
383	2:32	Vanessa, 5/6 cf 4/5	She thinks that they are equal because if you add 1 to each numerator, it equals the denominator. PSTs work with her, using a PDA to help her see that 5/6 > 4/5.	F	5th	Latino	comparison, fractions	scaffolding, extension question	misconstrued strategy, misconception	intermediate, wrong answer, technology	0383 at 013.jpg
384	2:29	Vanessa, compares fractions	She uses a variety of strategies to compare fractions.	F	5th	Latino	comparison, fractions		misconstrued strategy, misconception	intermediate, wrong answer	0384 at 227.jpg
385	1:30	Vanessa, converts 2-3/5	She shades partitioned circles to solve.	F	5th	Latino	renaming fractions, fractions		drawing, number sense	intermediate	0385 at 050.jpg
386	2:08	Vanessa, decimal assessment	To compare decimals, she chooses the larger number without regard to the location of the decimal point. She recognizes that 1.8 is larger than .18 because it has one whole. She adds decimal numbers correctly.	F	5th	Latino	decimal addition, comparison, decimals		standard algorithm, procedure, misconstrued strategy, misconception	intermediate, wrong answer	286 at 215 in Select 08.jpg
387	1:26	Vanessa, writes 10 hundredths	She writes 10/100 and 1/10 in decimal form as .010	F	5th	Latino	renaming fractions, fractions, decimals		manipulatives	intermediate, wrong answer	0387 at 126.jpg
388	2:31	Megan & Donna, 4.7 cf 4.70	If they cannot add zeros to compare decimals, 4.70 > 4.7. Their misconceptions are further illustrated in their base-10-block representations of decimal numbers.	F	5th	Caucasian	comparison, decimals	extension question, probing	manipulatives, misconception	intermediate, wrong answer	0388 at 205.jpg
500	7:15	Cathy's class	Students explain solution strategies. A worm was at the bottom of a 13-foot hole. He started to climb out at 12:00 p.m. He climbed 3 feet/hour, then rested 1 hour and slid back 1 foot. This pattern continued. What time did he reach the top?	M, F	5th	Multi	story problem	whole class, student discourse, clarify, probing	patterns, drawing	intermediate	0500 at 306.jpg

CLIP #	TIME	TITLE	DESCRIPTION	GENDER	GRADE	ETHNICITY	CONTENT	TEACHING / INTERVIEWING	STRATEGY	MISC	SCREEN CAPTURE NAME
501	14:43	Cinzia's class, 25 × 10, 180 ÷ 10	Teacher facilitates children's thinking while they solve and share strategies for two story problems.	M/F	2nd	Multi	whole number multiplication, whole number division, story problem, place value, money	small group, student discourse, conceptual instruction, probing, extension question	direct modeling, manipulatives, skip counting, drawing, number sense	primary, teacher reflection/ advice	501 at 855 in Select 18.jpg
502	2:42	Elsie, CGI changed her teaching	The same pressures teachers face today existed 25 years ago. You need to have faith in a student's ability to problem solve. The problem-solving environment changes the nature of your relationship to the child.	F	Adult/ PST	African American				teacher reflection/ advice	none
503	1:30	Elsie, challenges	Asking the right question was her greatest challenge. She believes that problem solving equalized the playing field. It provided equal access for all students.	F	Adult/ PST	African American				teacher reflection/ advice	none
504	2:30	Elsie, how/why	New teachers should be unafraid to stray from textbooks. Students have more and more important knowledge than is tested. Strategies developed through problem solving serve them better and for a longer period of time than drill.	F	Adult/ PST	African American			invented strategy	teacher reflection/ advice	none
505	0:56	Elsie, the one best strategy	When asked why she could not just teach the one best strategy, she replies that not everyone learns in the same way.	F	Adult/ PST	African American				teacher reflection/ advice	none
506	3:43	Elsie, typical lesson	She started with calendar activities. She realized the importance of counting. Word problems set in a familiar context provided students opportunities to develop and share various strategies.	F	Adult/ PST	African American	counting	student discourse	invented strategy	teacher reflection/ advice	none

CLIP #	TIME	TITLE	DESCRIPTION	GENDER	GRADE	ETHNICITY	CONTENT	TEACHING / INTERVIEWING	STRATEGY	MISC	SCREEN CAPTURE NAME
507	5:29	Fraction kids, 4 share 5	Four children discuss their answers to 5 shared by 4. One child counts aloud 1/4, 2/4, 3/4, 4/4, and 5/5. Teacher helps him see that it should be 5/4. One child is not sure how to name 5/4. Teacher asks whether 5/4 and $1\frac{1}{4}$ are the same amount.	M, F	2nd	Multi	fractions, equal sharing, story problem, whole number division, role of the unit, renaming fractions	small group, student discourse, scaffolding	drawing, direct modeling, misconception	primary	0507 at 325.jpg
508	9:01	Fraction kids, 8 shared by 6	Children draw and share solutions. One child thinks that each person gets $1\frac{2}{6}$; another answers $1\frac{1}{3}$. Another answers $1\frac{2}{6}$. They decide that both get the same amount but in different ways.	M, F	2nd	Multi	fractions, equal sharing, story problem, whole number division, renaming fractions	small group, student discourse, scaffolding	drawing, direct modeling	primary, Exceptional Reasoning	0508 at 420.jpg
509	3:19	Fraction kids, mixed/improper	Four children explore the concept of improper fractions with apples. Teacher asks how many eighths are in all the apples in front of them. Teacher asks how many whole apples. How many eighths are in one apple? Two apples? Three apples?	M, F	2nd	Multi	fractions, equal sharing, story problem, role of the unit	small group, student discourse, scaffolding	direct modeling, manipulatives	primary	0509 at 139.pct
510	6:01	Fraction kids, naming w/ doughnuts	Four children explore, with their teacher, the meaning of fractions and how we name them. They use doughnuts to model.	M, F	2nd	Multi	fractions, role of the unit, identifying fractions	small group, student discourse, scaffolding	direct modeling, manipulatives	primary	0510 at 231.jpg
511	1:18	Fraction kids, naming w/manip	Four children explore, with their teacher, the meaning of fractions and how we name them. They use fraction circles to model.	M, F	2nd	Multi	fractions, role of the unit, identifying fractions	small group, student discourse, scaffolding	direct modeling, manipulatives	primary	0511 at 022.jpg
512	2:44	Fraction kids, sizes & pieces	Four children discuss, with their teacher, the sizes of pieces in relation to the number of pieces in the whole.	M, F	2nd	Multi	fractions, role of the unit, identifying fractions	small group, student discourse, scaffolding		primary	0512 at 133.jpg

133

CLIP #	TIME	TITLE	DESCRIPTION	GENDER	GRADE	ETHNICITY	CONTENT	TEACHING / INTERVIEWING	STRATEGY	MISC	SCREEN CAPTURE NAME
513	3:24	Summing Integers	After exploring summing 1 to 10 and 1 to 20, a similar problem, teacher asks students to sum the numbers from 1 to 100. He asks whether they can write a rule for that? A fourth grader shares her rule.	M, F	4th	Multi	algebra	whole class, student discourse	patterns	intermediate	none
514	8:37	Jen & Sharon reflection	Two teachers discuss how they implement problem solving in their 1st-grade classes.	F	Adult/ PST	Caucasian	place value	whole class		teacher reflection/ advice	none
515	7:27	Jen's class, 4 × 11	Teacher presents a problem to the class: "If there are 11 seeds in each pack, how many seeds are in 4 packs?" Video clip shows children solving and sharing strategies with the class and one another. Four students share their strategies.	M, F	1st	Multi	whole number multiplication, story problem	whole class, student discourse, probing, conceptual instruction, extension question	direct modeling, drawing, manipulatives, hundred chart, fingers, counting on	primary	0515 at 447.jpg
516	4:29	Julie's class, 30 ÷ 5	Teacher presents a problem to the class: "There are 5 people and 30 stickers. How many stickers does each person get?" Video clip shows children sharing strategies with the class.	M, F	1st	Multi	whole number division, story problem, equal sharing	whole class, student discourse, probing	direct modeling, drawing, manipulatives	primary	0516 at 428.jpg
517	6:30	June & Maryann visit the CMTE	Two veteran teachers who teach mathematics conceptually discuss their journeys and answer questions from PSTs.	F	Adult/ PST	Caucasian		conceptual instruction		teacher reflection/ advice	none
518	7:38	June's class, conceptual lesson	She uses pattern blocks as a vehicle to teach converting between mixed numbers and improper fractions. Through exploring the relationships among the blocks, notation, and language, students begin to create their own understanding and algorithms.	M, F	5th, 6th	Multi	fractions, renaming fractions	whole class, conceptual instruction, scaffolding, student discourse, wait time, extension question	direct modeling, drawing, manipulatives, invented strategy	intermediate	0518 at 142.jpg

134

CLIP #	TIME	TITLE	DESCRIPTION	GENDER	GRADE	ETHNICITY	CONTENT	TEACHING / INTERVIEWING	STRATEGY	MISC	SCREEN CAPTURE NAME
519	5:58	June's class, procedural lesson	She teaches how to convert between mixed numbers and improper fractions using the standard algorithms.	M, F	5th, 6th	Multi	fractions, renaming fractions	whole class, procedural instruction, wait time	procedure, standard algorithm	intermediate	0519 at 445.jpg
520	3:17	Maryann, 192,000 discussion	A teacher facilitates a child's thinking while he attempts to explain why he thinks that 19,200 tens is another way to say 192,000.	M	3rd, 4th	Multi	place value	student discourse, whole class	number sense	primary, intermediate	520 at 350 in Select 19.jpg
521	6:34	Maryann, 251 × 12	Two students share their strategies for solving 251 × 12. Jacob says that it is 251 × 10 plus 251 × 2. Dani thinks that it is 250 × 10 plus 250 × 2 plus 1 × 12.	M, F	3rd, 4th	Multi	whole number multiplication, place value	student discourse, whole class	distributive property, composing/decomposing numbers, number sense	primary, intermediate	0521 at 357.pct
522	0:47	CMTE, estimate 9/10 + 7/8	A PST shares that she is surprised that a child could estimate 9/10 + 7/8 before the PST could estimate the sum.	F	Adult/PST	Caucasian	fraction addition, fractions	novice interviewer			none
523	3:15	Pam's class	Students share their solutions to a problem: "David wants to bring treats to class. He needs (35, 89, 106) treats. He has (15, 35, 74) treats already. How many more does he need?"	M, F	2nd	Multi	whole number addition, story problem, missing addend, whole number subtraction, place value	whole class, student discourse, probing	counting up, skip counting, composing/decomposing numbers, number sense	primary	0523 at 107.jpg
524	8:02	Peggy's class, Handies	A K/1 teacher explains how she uses "Handies" to teach base four. Video clip includes classroom footage and a discussion with the teacher.	M, F	K, 1st	Multi	place value, counting, whole number addition	whole class, small group	manipulatives, fingers, direct modeling	primary, teacher reflection/advice	0524 at 556.jpg

CLIP #	TIME	TITLE	DESCRIPTION	GENDER	GRADE	ETHNICITY	CONTENT	TEACHING / INTERVIEWING	STRATEGY	MISC	SCREEN CAPTURE NAME
525	3:36	Sharon's class, 10 × 5	Teacher presents a problem to the class: If 10 children planted 5 seeds each, how many seeds did they plant in all? Children act out the problem because some think that the answer is 15.	M, F	1st	Multi	whole number multiplication, story problem	whole class, student discourse	drawing, direct modeling, fingers	primary	0525 at 331.jpg
526	7:55	Tonya's class	Teacher presents a problem to the class: "A concert costs $55. Tyler has 17 one-dollar bills, 13 half dollars, 16 quarters, 31 dimes, and 234 nickels. Does he have enough? Video clip shows students sharing their strategies.	M, F	3rd	Multi	whole number addition, whole number multiplication, story problem, money, whole number division, place value	whole class, student discourse, probing, clarify	repeated addition, drawing, skip counting	primary	0526 at 559.jpg
600	1:04	Arlene, interview introduction	Interviewer begins an interview.	F	1st	Latino		introducing interview		primary	none
601	3:14	Bryce	For 5 + 3, child says that he knows it in his brain. He knows 4 + 7 because he's smart. For 14 − 5, he says 6. Interviewer asks him to count with blocks and to hand him the blocks while he counts. When asked how many are left, child says 0.	M	2nd	Caucasian	whole number addition, whole number subtraction, story problem	difficult interview, scaffolding	manipulatives, direct modeling	wrong answer, primary	0601 at 236.jpg
602	0:54	Jamie, interview introduction	Jamie and Sara (PSTs) introduce the interview with Andrew. PST asks him to show how high he can count.	F	Adult/ PST	Caucasian		introducing interview		primary	none
603	0:53	Julie (PST) with Michael	When he compares fractions by circling the larger fraction correctly, the PST does not ask how he knows.	M	5th	Caucasian	fractions, comparison	novice interviewer		intermediate	0603 at 047.jpg

136

CLIP #	TIME	TITLE	DESCRIPTION	GENDER	GRADE	ETHNICITY	CONTENT	TEACHING / INTERVIEWING	STRATEGY	MISC	SCREEN CAPTURE NAME
604	1:00	Justin, interview introduction	Justin (PST) introduces the interview with Mike. PST asks him to show how high he can count.	M	Adult/PST	Caucasian		introducing interview		primary	none
605	1:27	Lala, interview introduction	Lala (PST) introduces the interview with Stephanie. PST talks to the child about the interview to help make the child feel comfortable.	F	Adult/PST	Multi		introducing interview		primary	605 at 114 in Select 20.jpg
606	3:41	Nicole, interview introduction	Interviewer talks to the child about the interview to help make the child feel comfortable.	F	2nd	Caucasian	counting	introducing interview		primary	606 at 318 in Select 21.jpg
607	8:13	Richard	He solves 4 + 12, directly modeling with blocks incorrectly; 14 – 5, directly modeling with blocks incorrectly; 6 + ? = 13, directly modeling with blocks incorrectly, but then recounts; 5 × 3 using his fingers.	M	2nd	Caucasian	whole number addition, whole number subtraction, counting, story problem, missing addend, whole number multiplication	wait time, difficult interview, probing, clarify	manipulatives, direct modeling, counting on, fingers	primary, wrong answer	0607 at 713.jpg